CHARLEY'S WORLD

CHARLEY'S WORLD

◆

TRUE RECOLLECTIONS OF A JINXED MAN

Charles Barron

iUniverse, Inc.
New York Lincoln Shanghai

CHARLEY'S WORLD
TRUE RECOLLECTIONS OF A JINXED MAN

Copyright © 2006 by Charles Barron

iUniverse books may be ordered through booksellers or by contacting:

iUniverse
2021 Pine Lake Road, Suite 100
Lincoln, NE 68512
www.iuniverse.com
1-800-Authors (1-800-288-4677)

ISBN-13: 978-0-595-38001-5 (pbk)
ISBN-13: 978-0-595-82372-7 (ebk)
ISBN-10: 0-595-38001-8 (pbk)
ISBN-10: 0-595-82372-6 (ebk)

Printed in the United States of America

Contents

INTRODUCTION

The *first* day of my life was sixty-one years ago when I was born in a hospital delivery room in The Bronx, New York. That is the last normal thing I have done. The only reason there were no problems associated with my birth, was that most of the effort was out of my control.

Allow me to explain! My life is consistent with one of the most famous characters in American history, Joe Btfsplk. If you need to be reminded, Joe was the forlorn, bedraggled, jinxed resident of Dog Patch, a neighbor of Lil' Abner. Joe always had a rainy cloud over his head; it followed him everywhere. So here I am; it is undeniably true that my existence to date has been a symphony of personal disasters, faux pas and miscues. No matter if I am screwing in a light bulb or mowing the lawn; whether I travel around the corner or around the world; whether I am putting out the garbage or having a baby, something will go wrong. The simplest tasks for Mr. John Q. Normal have extraordinary, lasting, and newsworthy results under my care.

For the last 40+ years, innumerable such events have occurred straining both my luck and physical well being. However, something good did come from this string of ill fortune. After years of recounting such stories at parties to the gleeful reaction of the audiences, I started committing them to paper, and to my surprise, various newspapers around the country starting printing them as columns. The following "book" is actually a compilation of these columns which represent a glimpse into my life. These are by no means the totality of stupidity I have exhibited, but present a well balanced tour of the many twists and turns life has taken me.

For example, all of a sudden, I am sitting in Moscow, Russia, in a dark, dirty, interrogation room, in front of a very frightening customs agent and not really knowing if this will be the *last* day of my life. How does a nice Jewish boy from the U.S., a boring accountant no less, find himself under arrest in the Soviet Union, with his underwear full of $100 bills? Later, in a running gun battle through the streets of Moscow, hanging out of a cab door while Russian officials are shooting at us. What strange events have come together to make this all happen?

The stories are loosely chronological, but are arranged more by topic than by time and space. The "kids" in the stories are now full grown and off on their own. Scott, my oldest at 29 is a school basketball coach in Virginia, Tara at 26 is an accountant and the mother of a two year old. (Yes, I am a grandfather.) And Drew, the youngest at 19, is in college and while still living with Karen and me, still is an active participant in new calamities as they present themselves.

The stories I will relate are true. The names have not even been changed to protect the innocent. The adventures have not been exaggerated as the facts are colorful enough. To truly understand the set of cosmic forces which convened to cause my plight, one must understand the life path I have traveled and suffered. One must have studied the region between the ridiculous and the sublime, the zone between adventure and chaos. See the signpost up ahead; you are entering the chaos known as 'Charley's World.'

1

AN AMERICAN YANKEE IN KING BORIS' COURT

As the wheels of the Delta Airline's 747 hit the runway with a bone-jarring thud, I awoke from a fitful sleep. I was returning to my accounting job in Moscow after a short home leave, and I was nervous about the little secret I had in my pants.

After any other flight anywhere else in the world, I would have been pulling my luggage from the overhead as the wheels touched the ground. I would have stood impatiently in front of the sealed door waiting for the ramp to be rolled up. But as the plane rolled to a halt, I remained where I was—curled up under a mixed pile of empty peanut wrappers, dog-eared magazines, and a half eaten, beef stick Delta airlines jokingly calls a 'snack.' I was not eager to leave the security of my six-inch seat in the *cattle-car* coach section. Better to remain in my fetal position than face what came next.

I knew, and dreaded what awaited me—the infamous Russian customs and visa agents. Of all the situations, people, and places I had encountered during two years of working in Russia, *"the Evil Empire"*, nothing was like an arrival or departure from Moscow's major airport.

Just outside the door and lining the boarding ramp was a dozen or so armed, uniformed men and women. At least I think some were women. Sometimes the distinctions were not that clear, and the uniforms were of no help. It was hard to know who was what—army, militia, police, or just arrogant porters. Usually the porters just carried pistols. Russian porters are the only porters in the world to carry guns. They are also the only porters who are "always" tipped.

Faced everywhere with uniforms, automatic weapons and humorless expressions, I made my way into the terminal and melted into the crowd trying to look as inconspicuous as possible. The key to a speedy exit from the airport is not drawing any attention to oneself. For me, that meant shuffling along hunched forward, head down, eyes to the floor and hands in my pockets. Suitably stooped, I took up my position in the back of the customs line at Sheremetyevo Airport.

Sheremetyevo Airport is a monument to Communism. It is a sparse, no frills terminal, with glass walls everywhere. The glass architecture is not so you can see out, but so you can be seen from everywhere. One thing you give up in Russia is any semblance of privacy. Even where you think people would not want to know what your doing, they are in your face,....with a vengeance. Once, standing in front of a urinal, quietly minding my business, doing my thing, a cleaning lady walked in. You could tell she was a cleaning lady by her gray, permanent rumpled, summer/winter/formal/casual/one-size-fits-all dress. On her head was a kerchief. All Russian women wear kerchiefs. It's stapled on their heads at birth.

This cleaning lady was pushing a rolling slop sink containing enough black water to fill the Brooklyn aquarium, and a mop big enough to swab a Howitzer. She was there to clean and nothing or no one was going to stop her.

Treating me like just another porcelain fixture, she mumbled something in Russian and proceeded to mop the floors around me, including my shoes. The water was so thick and black I left with a fairly good shine. Embarrassed, but looking sharp, I headed for Russian immigration. It is always important to look your best as you enter immigration hell.

I was once again standing in line at dreaded passport control. The Russian agents would check my passport, stamp it and allow me to enter the country. There was a mob of 1500 exhausted and terrified travelers fearfully huddled behind a faded yellow line painted on the floor, waiting to present themselves to Russian customs clerks. The agents stand inside six subway-style token booths. The large room, designed to hold only one hundred people, is kept at a constant and comfortable ninety-six degrees.

This mob of passengers is on its own to merge into the six lines. As this herd moves slowly forward as a moving mass, you see people from many different countries. Packed closely in an overheated building, you quickly learn than in some countries bathing is only a holiday event.

After about an hour, I worked my way up to the yellow line. The line was not to be crossed without an overt *invitation* by the visa clerk. I learned the importance of the yellow line on my first visit when I stepped across it without invitation. Have you ever noticed how large the barrel of an AK-47 is when it's inches from you nose? I quickly learned to be an obedient horse at the gate and wait for the starting bell.

When my time came, the official in the booth suspiciously studied the face of this poor, stooped soul, cringing in front of her. It seems that no matter how long it actually takes to assure themselves that the documentation is proper, the procedure manual must designate a minimum required time. They stare at each page for minutes, before turning it to discover another page which requires even closer scrutiny. This is all done with nerve-wracking formality. U.S. State Motor Vehicle and Unemployment Departments often recruit these Russian officials as trainers.

I knew my passport and visa were both in order, so I had nothing to fear. I had pushed the documents through the small slit in the glass window and into the waiting hands of the female agent. She was a beady eyed, hawkish looking bureaucrat from her wire rimmed glasses to her hair bun tied so tight she would take off like a helicopter if it came loose. I knew-as the manual demanded—she would spend the next five minutes staring at my passport but to my surprise, after about thirty seconds of looking at my visa, she slid it back. "This is not the photograph of a living person," she announced.

I stood there in amazement. I knew my picture was bad, but being accused of using a morgue shot of a cadaver was downright insulting.

I stared back and her and tried to look calm. My mind raced. What can I say? What can I do? *What if she looks at my shoes?* Meekly, I tried to explain;

- I was sick when I had the passport photo taken.
- The photographer used bad lighting,
- Passport photos were always supposed to be unflattering.

- Yes, it did look strange, but indeed, it was me, and I was quite alive.

By now, one of those well-armed soldiers wandered over to see what the holdup was. The customs agent explained her accusation—that the man in the photo was a corpse. Taking my visa, the soldier held it next to my face studying both closely. I tried to suck in my cheeks. Then I tightened every muscle in my face to drain the blood out, trying to obtain the same pallor of me in the photo. I half-closed my eyes. There was nothing else to do but try to look dead. The solider looked at me and then the photo and then me again. "No, this is not good," he said. "This is a dead body lying down. Not you…..not you."

Looking around, I saw that most other visa operations had ceased. Everyone was now watching my little drama unfold. It was a Russian version of a Paine Webber commercial.

As a last ditch effort, I crossed my arms on my chest, closed my eyes, and leaned back as if lying down. Squinting to see what was happening, I saw the visa agent leaning forward staring at my face and body in its almost perpendicular stance. Some spectators told me later they thought I was in some sort of religious prayer position, and was going to attempt levitation.

Soon I heard the comforting sound of a stamp hitting my passport. The agent pushed the paperwork back to me shaking her head signifying she was still not 100% convinced I was alive, but unwilling to pursue it any further. I quickly picked up the documents and headed to customs clearance, knowing I was no longer just another face in the crowd.

Customs clearance entering Russia was designed for one purpose, to provide Customs agents with stuff to take home. There are so many things on the contraband list that gets confiscated; they probably don't even pay these guys. They just let them shop.

I was x-rayed three times and my bags were x-rayed three times. I would probably be able to read in bed without a nightlight from the major jolts of unprotected x-rays I had been exposed to. But it wouldn't hurt the money. Oh yea, the money. That's the real focus of this story.

I allowed myself to be placed in the unique position of smuggling fifteen thousand dollars in one hundred dollar bills as a favor for my Russian driver, Chenya. The U.S. Government was changing to a new $100 bill, and his savings for a new car was in the old bills, so he needed them converted. In Russia, however, U.S. hard currency is illegal, old or new. But I was I was up to my eyeballs in hard currency and facing Boris, the Customs man. I was nervous!

When I said I was 'up to my eyeballs' in hard currency, in reality I was several degrees of latitude off. Knowing the scrutiny I would be under, I had to find a safe place to hide my *booty*. Before leaving the plane I hid my fifteen packages of ten $100 bills in the safest place I could come up with. I hid my *stash*, in *my* stash. I packed them right into my Fruit of the Looms

So there I was, a New York born, dull accounting type, short, overweight, with such cat-like instincts that I once was run over by a car being pushed by two guys. I was walking towards one of the nastiest-looking customs agents I have ever seen in a country where jailing Americans is almost a custom. My shorts are packed full of illegal, contraband, hard currency, in an amount that, if discovered, would have me at a cocktail party with a KGB agent, who would make this guy look like Billy Graham.

So, what happens then? As I am walking, I feel movement in my shorts and it's not biological. Two of the packets—one in each leg—start sliding down. I smile, clamp my knees together, take a deep breath and saunter right up to Boris's counter.

Boris was a squat, ugly man, with a pock marked face, bloodshot eyes, a beet red face, and he was sweating profusely. *There was something dreadfully familiar about Boris, and then it hit me. I had seen this face before; once years ago, on a blind date.*

I stood nervously in front of Boris' steel desk covered with papers, while he finished what I think was his lunch. I say *think* as it was an assortment of fish heads, chicken beaks, and claws and some other indistinguishable body parts of animals I did not recognize. But he ate with gusto and washed it down with the obligatory swigs from a bottle of vodka. I hoped a full belly and a clouded head would make him miss the *package* I had hidden in my pants. Soon, he stopped chewing, burped and wiped his mouth with his sleeve. Taking my passport between two greasy fingers he looked up at me. "Mr. Charles, what are you bring-ing into my country?"

I was dead! Somehow they knew and I began racing through all the reasons why my pants were stuffed with money. "Mr. Charles, look at this x-ray!"

He held up the x-rays taken earlier. I saw two things immediately; I needed a root canal, and there was a stack of magazines neatly piled in one of my suitcases. "Mr. Charles, what kind of propaganda are you bringing in to Moscow?" he asked.

As he spoke, he started piling my bags up on the counter. One by one, he opened them until finally he found the one he was looking for; the one with the dangerous propaganda; the ones with naked girls on the cover; the ones called Playboy.

Boris began salivating again as soon as he picked them up. "These are contra-band, and you cannot take them into Moscow. They must be destroyed...destroyed," Boris said as he stamped my visa and motioned me to leave

As I looked back, I saw him stuffing the magazines into his pants.

2

MORE BOLSHOI AND
SOME BUDAPEST

I discovered very quickly during my first visit to a Russian supermarket that I would be on an enforced, low calorie diet. A TV-style dinner was $12.00, a head of lettuce, $9.00, and a bag of chips was $6.00. Eating with the same unencumbered gusto I have been accustomed to all my life would be a thing of the past. With limited selections, my eating habits changed from my trademark piranha-like frenzy, to a nibbling goldfish. But after living for a week on Pringles and Fanta orange soda, my body began telling me I needed a more diverse diet. To my surprise, I developed an unnatural desire for a bowl of corn flakes

I had never considered cold cereal as a meal, but suddenly I started having dreams of Corn Pops, Cheerios and Sugar Smacks. I fantasized of wallowing in a tub of Post Toasties. There were even mildly erotic thoughts involving shredded wheat, strawberries, and Tony the Tiger. The signs were plain—I desperately needed roughage.

My weekly trip to the supermarket in search of cereal was frustrated by cost. The cheapest of my fantasy items, common corn flakes, were $9 a box. My biological needs were suppressed by my frugal side, however. In other words, I was cheap. I could not bring myself to pay $9 for a box of cereal. I was too cheap to fulfill my desires, which has been the story of my life.

Feeling hungry and depressed, I was heading to the checkout counter with dinner—a Zag-Nut bar and mineral water—when I spotted a box of cereal for only $2.50. Although completely in German, the package had on it the easily identifiable and healthy name, "Mueslix" Even better was a picture of a big ceramic dish filled with grain, coconut and fruit. I was ecstatic. I purchased a container of Finnish milk and raced home, and for the next three days I had Mueslix for breakfast and dinner. It was better than sex, and a lot cheaper. I reveled in my bargain.......until the morning of the fourth day.

Waiting for my driver that morning, I decided to have a second bowl of my ambrosia. I was sitting there eating happily when my housekeeper, Olga, arrived. The classic Western image of Russian woman, she was like Hulk Hogan in drag. And, like every other Russian woman, Olga had a kerchief permanently affixed to her head.

Already of the opinion that Americans are several stars short of a full flag, Olga never blinked an eye no matter what she saw me doing. However bizarre my behavior, Olga would go about her duties as if nothing unusual was happening, but this time, she pulled up short after seeing me hunched over my bowl of Mueslix. Without a word she came to the table, put on her glasses and picked up the box for a closer look. Although she spoke no English, Olga did manage with two words to convey a message to me that all the German on the box could not; "Tweet, tweet!" Pointing at the box she repeated, "Tweet, tweet."

Suddenly I understood. For three days, seven meals, eight bowls-full in all, I had been eating bird food. I panicked. I was terrified that I had ingested some chemicals designed to keep my feathers shiny, and my droppings solid. Within hours I was at an American Clinic ready for the worst. Instead, I was told there was no real danger from eating birdseed, but corn flakes, however expensive, were probably better.

Relieved, I went home. True to the clinic's diagnosis, I never suffered any ill effects from my unusual diet, but it did take a week or so before I lost the impulse to hang around statues, and Olga resumed her studied indifference to my odd behavior. I did, however, always have a song on my lips.

It was shortly after the bird seed episode that my family flew to Moscow for a visit. I was more than happy to see them as Russia can be a lonely and confusing place. I was hoping everything would go perfectly, and I could convince my wife and family to stay. Of course, several "incidents" shattered that hope! After some minor sightseeing, we decided to go to the 'big one,' the 'Big Kahuna' of tourist spots in Russia.

Lenin's Tomb sits to one side of Red Square. Lenin was the leader of the Russian Revolution. His marble and concrete tomb looks like a museum except for the perpetual line of machine gun-laden soldiers watching the perpetual line of visitors waiting to get in. I never quite understood the need for soldiers. What did they think would be stolen? An 80-year-old waxen corpse is hardly a target of jewel or art thieves.

This particular frosty morning in February with the temperature hovering around 5 degrees, we decided to go and visit Lenin. As Russian winters go, this was beach weather and called for an outing. When we told my then 16-year-old daughter, Tara, we were going to Lenin's Tomb, she could not disguise her excitement. "I always liked the Beatles." So much for the Tennessee educational system!

Arriving at the mausoleum, we were greeted by a line ½ mile long. In 5 degree weather, I did not relish the thought of standing for hours in the slow-moving line. When I first arrived in Russia, I had been told that if you were an American and showed your passport to the guards, you would be allowed to go to the front of the line. So despite the protestations of my daughter and my 9-year-old son, Drew, we marched past hundreds of local Russians. The heavily armed guards looked cold and in a foul mood, but the expectation was that they would welcome, with open arms, a family of fat-cat, American tourists wearing 15 pound survival down coats recently purchased at Abercrombie & Fitch, and prepared to pay their respects to Lenin. After a brief exchange we were marching back to the end of the line which had grown even longer in our short absence. So much for détente and internationalism.

An hour later we finally made it to the front door and back to the same soldiers who almost pistol-whipped me when I suggested that I should be allowed to break line. As I walked through the massive steel doors, my continual talking to my wife, Karen, further annoyed the guards. Talking and keeping my frozen hands in my pockets was too much for the soldiers who had not forgotten my unsuccessful passport ploy.

In an outburst of Russian that needed no translation, we were told, "You inconsiderate pigs…show respect!"

Cold and chastised we entered the main rotunda. The interior was pitch black except for a spotlight on the casket. It was dark, cold, and extremely quiet with only the sound of organ music, and the shuffling of feet as visitors descended five steps to the casket level.

My five steps, still shaken from my public berating and unable to adjust immediately to the dark, made me do something which should put me in the ugly American Hall of Fame. I tripped down the stairs, flew across the room, and hit the casket broadside, hard enough to make Lenin shake!!!

After crashing into the casket, things—bad things-happened quickly.. They were like roaches with the lights on! It was as if Lenin had an alarm up his ass. Out of nowhere they came, dozens of soldiers, militia and police. I was literally lifted up off my feet and taken out the back of the tomb. I thought for sure they were going to put me up against a wall and shoot me. Then I saw Karen, Tara and Drew, surrounded by six soldiers and being marched out along side me. Looking into Karen's face I couldn't tell which reaction was stronger. Was it the stark terror of thinking she was going to be summarily executed, or the cold, steely conviction that if she did get out of this alive she would have her revenge? I don't know which I feared worse, what the soldiers would do to me now, or what Karen would do to me later.

After lining us up against a rear wall, they began motioning to us with their rifles. Not ever being really good at charades, I had no idea what they wanted. I thought it was either to take my pants off or dance around. Finally Karen figured it out. All along the rear wall were the tombs of every former Russia premier except Nikita Khrushchev. As a punishment for my missteps, they were demanding we pay homage to each one, right down the line. And so we did. Ah, Chachenko; ah Breznov; Ah! Ah! Ah! Whether we knew them or not, whether they were dead or not, we stopped at each grave, mumbled some garbled prayer with a Russian suffix and moved on. We shuffled down the line until our armed tour guides decided we had had enough and returned to Lenin. Fearing they might return, we ran like thieves. We raced around the building and disappeared as best we could into the crowds in Red Square. For anyone else, this would have been a harrowing experience. For us it was just another day of sightseeing for the Barrons.

Their little adventure did not stop here. Little did I know that a kidnapping incident would turn my family's first visit to this magic land of caviar and Cossacks into their last. It happened this way…

Olga, the housekeeper who pointed out that I was eating canary canapés, was also my landlord. To earn extra money, she also cleaned the apartment and did our laundry, a fact, which had a direct bearing on the case of the strange abduction.

Because of my employer's cash flow problems, Olga had not been paid her $4000 per month for over three months. Upset over the back-rent, Olga decided to bring some attention to my firm's financial short-comings. Unfortunately, the action Olga took was not through the legal system. There were no persistent demands for money, or a 300-pound goon with a stick of wood. My landlady was too clever for that.

Instead, Olga decided the best way to get her money was to hold my family's laundry hostage. Sweat socks, jeans and pajama tops, shirts and skirts, three different sizes of jockey shorts, and assorted woman's paraphernalia were the victims. The ransom note's loose translation was: "Have my money here by Friday, or you will never see your underwear again."

My family was leaving on Thursday and my wife was despondent over this turn of events. We went on television pleading to the public to notify the authorities if they saw the bundle. I even contacted the elite *Fruit of the Loom URT* (*U*nderwear Recovery Team), but they turned me down because our things were from K-Mart.

After hours of negotiation led by a former KGB agent who worked for my company, it was agreed that half of the rent would be paid in exchange for return of my family's clothes. My things would remain hostage until full payment was made.

The exchange would later be made at the airport, and my family would return home with one more exciting story to tell their friends. I, on the other hand, had to wear two-week-old briefs until the third largest accounting firm in the world could come up with $4,000 to pay the ransom.

The time finally arrived for Karen and the kids to leave. It was an hour trip to the airport, and I planned on leaving my apartment at 6:00 A.M. Even though I had a very important breakfast meeting at 8:00 A.M. back in town, I decided to go with them figuring I could easily make it back in time for my meeting.

I had arranged for a large van to pick us up at 6:00 A.M. and I had everyone up at 5:00 A.M. to get ready. There were four of us with a substantial amount of luggage. There was enough luggage to turn the typical Russian cab into a circus clown.

At 6:00 A.M. there was no van. At 6:30 A.M., there was still no van and I began to get nervous. If they got to the airport late and missed their flight, their visas would expire. If their visas expired they literally could not leave the airport until the next available flight, be it a day or a week later. After the trauma of my own two previous episodes of being trapped in a Russian airport for a few days, I knew any jury would acquit my wife if she murdered me; Justifiable Homicide.

I ran down to the street and flagged the first taxi I saw. The four of us and the driver piled into the car but not before squeezing in enough luggage to have supported the Bulgarian Olympic Hockey team for a week. And off we went.

Using my innate 'American Savvy', I offered the driver an extra $50 if he made the one hour trip to the airport in forty five minutes. It was like the runaway train at Disneyland, but he made it. Huddled together in the car with all our baggage, I knew how the early astronauts felt. Well, except instead of a ground crew and 2,000 support personnel, we had a lunatic Russian driver named Igor.

We did get there about 7:30 A.M. cutting it very close. Knowing the experience of customs and passport control was as painful leaving as arriving, I was glad it was her and not me. However, my challenge now was to get back to town and to my meeting. Seeing that Igor did his job going to the airport, I decided to make him the same offer returning. Big mistake, big, big mistake.

It had now started snowing and the roads were icy. Even so, he decided he could still maintain his 90 mph pace, and even push it a little bit because he was losing time in the skidding, wheel spinning, and the sideswiping of cars and buildings.

In Moscow there is an occupation called a Gi'a. There are, in effect, traffic cops who stand on busy intersections. They stand outside a small booth-like office, wearing a uniform similar to an Italian constable, brandishing a long, white, stick. This *stick* is feared throughout Moscow.

If you are approaching one of them and all of a sudden he is wildly waving his stick in front of your car, you had better stop and you can be sure of a hefty, on-the-spot-fine. If you do not stop, the next one will hunt you down and the odds are you will never be seen again. Oddly, the majority of tickets are issued to Mercedes, Cadillac's, BMW's and Limousines. If they think there is a foreign businessman in a taxi, he is also fair game. These popular jobs are handed down from father to son. They are in the same union as the armed porters

We were flying down one particularly straight stretch of wide open road and Igor must have been doing 100 mph. All I saw was the white blur of snow, trees punctuated by the white sticks of the traffic cops. I had started out the trip in the back seat but I arrived in the front seat after Igor slammed on the brakes. A pair of traffic cops armed with their white sticks had finally cornered him.

Within seconds there was one Gi'a screaming in the front window at Igor, and one screaming at me on the passenger side. I had no idea why they thought I had anything to do with this crime. I guess since I was wearing a suit, and Igor was wearing a goatskin vest, I was the co-signer. They opened both doors and pulled us out and into their little, hut office.

Inside they placed us at two separate tables and the screaming continued. Igor just kept shrugging and pointing to me, and I just kept shrugging and asking for my one phone call to the America Embassy. My guy began an impersonation of Nikita at the U.N. and started pounding his fist on the table. Knowing the hygiene of local Russians, I was petrified he would take off his shoe.

Just as he appeared to be reaching for his foot, there was a loud crash outside. From the noise there had apparently been a serious car crash. The two Gi'as, probably thinking they could strip some jewelry off the bodies, shouted something at us, and ran out.

Suddenly, Igor began pulling me toward the door. The first thing that entered my mind was that if Igor escapes, and all they have is me, they will kill me, take my wallet, and in a few days I would pop up on the Moscow river like some well dressed buoy. I made a few quick calculations on my chances of going or staying, so I chose going. As we ran out the door towards the cab, we saw the Gi'as a few dozen feet up the road. What's worse is they saw us, and started running back. By now Igor was in the cab and starting to pull away. He had pushed open the passenger door, but did not wait for me to get in. I began running along the side the car trying to get my left leg in. Now if I would measure my athletic prowess on a scale from 1-10, I would have to go into some heavy training to hit the 1. I know people that run marathons, but I get winded driving twenty six miles. So with this as a reference point, my keeping up with the accelerating cab and getting my leg in was a huge accomplishment. By now our two captors had reached their car and were in hot pursuit. Seeing this, Igor did what any law-abiding Russian citizen would do, he sped up. Only a sharp left turn on two wheels pulled me into the car. Otherwise it was as if I was using the car as a skateboard all the way back to Moscow.

As our pursuers started catching up, I heard 'popping' noises coming from behind us. I thought the cab was backfiring. That is until the rear window exploded in pieces from a bullet. I huddled on the floor almost under the front seat shamelessly trying to save my ass. I felt the cab speed up and make wild rights and lefts through Moscow's backstreets.

They say at times like this your life flashes before your eyes, but nothing happened. Either my life to date was so boring, even to me, or I just could not focus on spooling it up. Either way no life playback materialized. However, the spectacle was so absurd, so strange, so bizarre, and so surreal, all I could think of the old Keystone Cops chases. But in those they only got a pie in the face when caught. Here I think the reward will be much harder and much more painful.

Sudden, the taxi slowed then squealed to a halt. I crawled out from under the dash and found myself in front of the National Hotel where my breakfast meeting was to be held. Standing above me, watching me extricate myself from the car, was the President of a major banking client of the firm with whom I was to breakfast. I stood up, dusted myself off, paid the driver and walked with as much dignity as I could muster into my meeting.

Was I embarrassed or surprised? Was I depressed? Are you kidding? It's just another day living in 'Charley's World.'

Igor's behavior was not really very Russian. One of the most obvious traits of the Russian people I've noticed is their inability most of the time to make quick decisions about anything. This indecisiveness was illustrated during my first few days at work. I arrived early one morning at a small conference room which was serving as my temporary office. A Russian clerk had made herself comfortable at the table I was using as a desk. She spoke no English and I could not explain to her that I needed the entire table for the meeting I was about to have. She just kept smiling and offering me tea.

I needed help so I called upon the 'Office Administrator' to translate. He went into the office and after about five minutes returned. "She says she has nowhere else to sit!" he said, then left.

"Not good enough," I thought to myself and went one rung up the chain of command to the 'Office Manager.'

He took ten minutes and returned with virtually the same response, "Someone is sitting at her desk and she has nowhere else to go."

By now the 'Office Administrator' had returned with the 'Head of Personnel,' and the 'Head of Security', a former KGB Officer, and a twenty-minute heated meeting ensued in the hallway. Finally, a representative of the delegation informed me that the woman could not be moved. He explained that they had nowhere else to put the squatter who had taken over the woman's desk. I was just out of luck and would have to share.

I decided to go straight to the top. I called 'Alla', the Managing Partner's secretary who was incredibly tough and scrappy even though she stood just her 4'5".

She stormed into the conference room and after saying only seven or eight words, my unwelcome guest packed up her papers and left.

"What did you say to her," I asked incredulously.

"I told her to get the hell out," she replied matter-of-fact reply.

Today's Russia is changing almost on a daily basis. The fall of the Soviet Union has given birth to the liberalization of various social, economic, human rights and legal forms with typical labor pains. However, real growth could be helped if the philosophy of hesitancy and uncertainty were replaced with decisiveness and individual thought and conceptualization.

It all goes back to the old saying, "A camel is a horse designed by a committee." During our early years in school, at least once per month we found ourselves under our desks, hiding our heads under our arms the old Duck and Cover drills of the Cold War. This was to train for the inevitable nuclear attack from the evil empire, the Soviet Union. If I knew then what I know now, I would have stayed at my desk and read a comic book. They can't even get a passenger aircraft to stay in the air, let alone a missile. Here's how I know.

On a recent trip to Prague in the Czech Republic, I had the opportunity to fly an airline which is fast becoming a legend in its own time, Aeroflot, the National Airline of Russia. Television magazine shows had broadcast episodes describing chickens running in their aisles and pilots napping. Newspaper articles had depicted decrepit planes and defective equipment. The U.S. Federal Aviation Administration has called it the "worst airline in the world."

Armed with that knowledge, I swore that during my temporary assignment in Moscow, I would never, ever, fly this airline. However, as usual, fate had other ideas.

To get from the Czech Republic back to Russia I had only one choice unless I was willing to wait three days. It was Aeroflot or twiddle my thumbs for seventy two hours, and then try to explain the delay to the bosses. I decided that my boss was far more dangerous than the flight, so I purchased a one way ticket to Moscow on Aeroflot. As often happens in Charley's world, I had chosen wrong!

The flight was scheduled to leave Prague at 2:00 P.M. As was my custom, I arrived promptly at 11:30 A.M. so I could avoid any crowds. Oddly, my company had agreed to purchase a First Class seat. I was guessing they thought there was a possibility that this could be my last flight.

After clearing passport control, I turned into the main terminal where I faced a line of two hundred Russian tourists returning to Moscow on the same flight. There were so many boxes, bags, packages and bundles it looked like a war-time evacuation. But not to worry, I thought. I would be in first class.

I searched the check-in counters for the first class window to no avail. I saw no oasis for us—*the preferred people.* "Of course, there must be one," I thought to myself and headed for a customer service representative. I showed him my ticket and then waited for him to pick up my bags and lead me past this throng, and into the First Class lounge, apologizing profusely for any inconvenience I had to endure.

"You will sit in the front of the plane," he gruffly instructed me in broken English, handing me back my ticket and leaving me in line as anonymous passenger # 201.

One hour later I boarded the aircraft. I had seat 2A in First Class and I couldn't wait to start enjoying my First Class experience. However, before I could start enjoying the experience, I would have to remove from my seat a 250-pound gentleman with a tattoo on his face. Showing him my ticket with '2A' prominently displayed helped not a bit, as he responded by holding up his own ticket with '2A.' The stewardess solved our problem quickly. She crossed out the 2A on my ticket and wrote in 7B.

I was now in Business Class and my hopes of a comfortable flight were fading fast. I abandoned what hope I had left when I saw sitting in row 7B the evil twin of my friend in 2A. I was now getting mad and I wanted action.

I raced up the aisle of the plane against the flow of boarders and found the steward. I immediately vented my frustrations of the past two hours. I had hardly begun my protestations when a sudden realization overtook me. The men in seats 2A and 7B were actually part of a family of triplets and I had just begun complaining to their larger brother.

"Shut up and sit down now!" he bellowed so loudly they must have heard him in the control tower. I turned and slinked my way to the rear of the plane to the last row in the back of the plane. I had gone from First Class to Business and now was in Coach.

I was tired, disgusted, and nervous about what might come next. So nervous I had to use the facilities before takeoff. I had almost half an hour before departure so it was no problem. There I sat finally enjoying some space and solitude when I felt the plane jerk. Paying no mind, I focused my attention to the matters at hand. I then felt the aircraft start to move and before I could extricate myself from my current surroundings, I heard the engines roar, the nose lift up and we were airborne. Obviously, the pilot felt we had enough people on board, or he had a date waiting back in Moscow. Whatever the reason we had departed almost half an hour early with me in the bathroom.

The ironic fact of the whole ridiculous situation was that despite my jockeying for the last forty five minutes for my seat, I really didn't even need one!

My brushes with death and chaos did not constrain itself to the Russian fatherland. My position required me to travel all over Eastern and Western Europe including London, Prague and Budapest. In fact, in Budapest, I created, what could be called, a minor international incident.

My first trip brought me to the Hyatt Hotel in Budapest. The Hyatt is a beautiful facility right on the banks of the Danube River. The Danube cuts through the city with Buda on the far bank, with its magical castles and Disneyland type structures, and Pesch, where the hotel sits.

On my first morning at the hotel, I dressed and went down to the lobby for a bite of breakfast before a long day of meetings. A very ornate and European styled hotel, the restaurant was beautifully appointed and very plush….and very crowded. Everyone had the same idea as I and had come in early. I was told by a very snooty and self-absorbed host that there was an hour wait. Not wanting to wait, I decided to grab something somewhere else. Walking out, I noticed just to the right another breakfast room. Being very pushy, I eased open the closed door and noticed immediately it was almost empty. A lone sign in Japanese was taped to the door; instructions I thought to some tour group.

A few guests sprinkled around the restaurant, but no maitre d'. Again, being bold I just wandered in and seated myself right at a window overlooking the Danube.

A beautiful site, relaxing, peaceful, but I was hungry. After ten minutes and with no waiter in view, I got up and started wandering around hoping to find a breakfast buffet. I found no buffet but I did find a beautiful omelet bar. A large steel cart with a hot grille, small glass containers of scallions, mushrooms, pickles and such was ready to go. There were plates, bowls and even a cauldron of hot water to boil the eggs, a la poached or hard boiled; very, very classy.

It had everything except eggs. I assumed I was early before the chef actually opened it up. But I am innovative, I am resourceful, I am an American. So, I wandered into the kitchen and after some translation problems liberated three eggs from a very confused kitchen staff. I headed back to the cart to make myself some breakfast.

Turning up the heat on the grill, I grabbed some scallions and other stuff and started frying them up before cracking my three prizes on the grille. Lacking a spatula, I grabbed a fork off a table and scrambled them up. There were no trash bags so I threw the shells into the boiling kettle. What a beautiful sight, the sizzling, bubbling mass of yellow and white eggs colored by all of the vegetables I had scrambled in. Cautious about using an egg covered fork, I washed off the fork carefully in the cauldron and was almost done. Looking behind me now, I was surprised to see a line of about twenty well dressed Asian gentlemen all waiting apparently to have omelets too. Directly behind me was an elderly man. I knew that without a chef he would probably have problems cooking so without a second thought I offered him my plateful of eggs. His reaction was unexpected. He began shouting at me, flailing his arms and in a wild and erratic manner started spitting on me. Soon, the others behind him joined in. I was completely dumbfounded. That is, until the room manager raced over, grabbed me by my collar and dragged me back into the hotel lobby. What had I done?

The *Omelet Mystery* solution

- The 'empty breakfast room' was being used as a private breakfast meeting room for the Japanese Trade Delegation to Hungary. That small sign explained this fact.

- The 'omelet bar' was their Miso Soup preparation table. I had rinsed my utensils and thrown my egg shells into their soup.

• Japanese hold grudges. They were very, very upset and have very good memories. They spat at me all week as they passed by me in the hotel lobby!

3

BLIND DATES, BLIND HORSES AND BLIND JUSTICE

Such occurrences as was befalling me in Russia, was in no way, shape, or form new to me. From as early as I can remember, my life has been under this edict from above. It is as if God issued an inter-office memo to his staff saying, "If we have to do anything strange to anyone, pick Charley, he won't be surprised or upset. He's expecting it!" And so it was, and so it would be. This was especially interesting during my dating days.

This time we were really trying to dazzle these girls. My friend, Jerry, and I both had blind dates and we knew fate was with us, because the girls were gorgeous. Joanne was blond, 5'5", and my dream girl. Denise, Jerry's date, was a clone, except that she was a brunette. We were both twenty, single, with raging hormones, and these were by far the best looking dates we ever had.

Neither Jerry nor I were what could be called Don Juans. I was 5'8", bespectacled, with acne, and had limited experience with girls. However, I was the better catch between the two of us. Jerry was 6'0,' chronically flat-footed (to the point of spontaneously falling down) and had a severe stammer. We were two dates for which any woman in her right mind would kill.

During my initial phone conversation with Joanne, I had, as usual, lied. I gave her story line #3b; that my father was an orthopedic surgeon and I always show my dates a good time. It was standard operating procedure in the early sixties to pre-sell yourself to your escort. It meant wasting less valuable date time on impressing, which then can be devoted to the more important activity of seducing. It goes without saying that Jerry's father was my father's partner in the practice. In reality, these girls were going out with the sons of a shoe salesman and a

23

press operator. Hardly glamour city, but the girls were excited, and that's exactly how we wanted to keep them.

Our current problem, however, was that we had a total budget of twenty-five dollars between us. You can't do too much jet setting on twenty five bucks. We were still pondering our problem the morning of the big date, when my mother walked in with the solution. The night before at a charity function, she had won a gift certificate for dinner for four at a very expensive nightclub in the city, *Manna from Mamma*. We were sure we were going to get lucky tonight.

Never to leave anything to fate, I decided to give Jerry a crash course in etiquette. Despite my lean dating experience, I had mastered the social graces, but Jerry still ate his salad with a spoon, lest he lose any dressing. I covered everything such as what fork to use, wine selection, table manners, and the works. Without a doubt, we were ready!

The big night arrived. We picked the girls up, and within thirty seconds they were suspicious. As we walked over to the Chevy Corvair I had to borrow, my Pinto was in the shop. Joanne asked, "Where's your Mazeratti?"

I had forgotten I told her I had one, and I also had forgotten to tell Jerry, who chimed in, "Yeah Charlie, I meant to ask you, where's the Maz?" He thought he was helping.

"It's in the shop. It's always in the shop. You know those German cars, always in the shop," I tried to cover. "I had to borrow this one from the house boy. Dad's got the Corvette." As we got in the car, I heard Joanne whisper to her friend "It looks like a converted motorcycle." I mumbled to Jerry, "We're in trouble!"

We arrived at the nightclub, and of course, there was valet parking. One of the attendants opened my door, handed me the receipt and then got behind the wheel, while another one opened the doors for the girls. I met the girls at the curb and started walking in. I looked around, no Jerry. Where the hell was Jerry? As I watched the car pull away, through the rear window, I saw Jerry still sitting in the back seat being driven with the car to some remote parking area. He had thought one of the attendants was going to open the door for him too. All I could think was, "What a great start!"

After a long walk from the parking area, Jerry joined us at our table. Things were not going well, but how much worse could they get? I was wrong.

The waiter came and handed us menus. "Can you suggest something?" Denise asked Jerry.

Jerry leaned over to me and whispered, "It's in French or something. I can't read it."

"You've got it upside down, moron," I whispered back.

Turning it right side up, he was still confused. To this point, if it was anything more expensive than White Castle, it was out of his league.

"Escargots, yum, one of my favorites," he told her.

I leaned over and said, "Snails, they're snails. Are you going to eat snails?"

His face turned pale. Continuing to read down the menu, he blurted out, "Mouse, too. What kind of place is this?"

"What a kidder," I told the now staring duo.

"Idiot, that's mousse, chocolate pudding. Just keep quiet, I'll order."

Seeing something on the menu I recognized, I told the waiter four orders of these, pointing to what I thought was a fish stew. "Yes sir," he responded, "Four orders of calves' brains with mustard sauce."

I had to leave. I excused myself to go to the men's room. I had to think. Not only did they think we weren't sophisticated, I also had the feeling they thought we were newly arrived immigrants. I had to think. Where best to think than in those little cubicles in the men's room designed especially for thinking. As I sat and considered the evening to that point, I had to laugh. The more I thought, the more I laughed, and soon I was roaring loudly.

Finally, someone sitting in the next booth asked me, "When your finished reading that, can I have it? It sounds really funny."

"I'm not reading anything," I confessed. Dead silence from the other booth, and I left quickly.

Returning to the table, I noticed the waiter had brought a large, silver tureen for each of us. It contained clear water with bright yellow slices of lemon floating on top. As I sat down, I winced. Jerry was very properly, pinkie up, spooning the contents of the tureen into his mouth, not even slurping. The girls and the waiter just watched quietly.

"Charley, try this. Cold lemon soup. Excellent, excellent."

"Anything for a joke," I pleaded, as I pulled the spoon out of his hand. "Why don't you put your hands in the finger bowl like everyone else? Stop this kidding."

I just wanted to go home. It was basically a quiet meal, everyone choking down their calves' brains. Finally, we were finished and were about to leave. The waiter had given Jerry the check, so I subtly slipped him the gift certificate. All he had to do was put the tip in and quietly hand it to the waiter.

"His mother won this thing, we don't pay anything," Jerry loudly informed the waiter. I wanted to go under the table.

"Yes sir, that's fine," the waiter answered.

"Can we go now?" Jerry wanted reassurance.

"That's up to you, sir. Thank you, gentlemen."

I ran for the car with everyone else in pursuit. I just wanted to be alone.

A long alleyway separated the parking lot from the main road. I raced up the alley, and made a squealing, sharp right onto the street. A hard bump, made me jam on the brakes. Looking out my window, I realized I was about twenty feet off the ground. I couldn't figure out where we were, until I opened my door and looked straight down to the street below. I had driven up a ramp to the top of a car carrier unloading automobiles at a local dealer. We were on the uppermost ramp. I just sat there. The girls were screaming at me, Jerry was laughing, and the driver of the transport was jumping up and down and cursing.

Actually, the rest of the evening is sort of a blank, but I do remember the only *luck* we had was ending the night with our lives.

This is how it has always been. This is how most of my life has gone. Not crazy, but slightly out of alignment. Not stupid, but not fully in sync with the rest of the world. I've always been right at the edge of being refined, but not quite there. I've always been Lemon Soup. This was not the only time Jerry and woman have come together to provide 'theater for the Gods.'

Blind dates, in general were always disastrous for us. On this one particular evening though, it was Jerry who had the blind date, and for only the second time in his life, she was gorgeous and he did not want to blow this one.

Jerry had a handicap that had plagued him for years; he stuttered. The more nervous he got, the more he stammered. On this night, on this blind date, he was very, very nervous. He had been trying all night to impress this goddess without really speaking. A combination of David Niven and Marcel Marceau, he seemed to be doing fine until we went to dinner.

There were four couples in our group. Jerry sat to my left with his date facing him. The place was a Chinese restaurant in Queens, New York. The waiter was Dong. He came for our orders.

Dong not only had problems with English, but he also had a hearing problem, which turned out to be hellish combination for Jerry. Dong started at the far end of the table two couples away from me and three away from Jerry. Jerry was watching the trouble the first couple was having ordering and he panicked. The last thing he needed was to have an extended conversation with a deaf, non-English speaking alien. He began practicing his order.

In order to avoid an extended discussion with the waiter, he selected a five syllable dinner, "Sliced chicken sandwich!" Simple, direct, no problem. He rehearsed, "Sliced chicken sandwich, sliced chicken sandwich," in an almost inaudible chant, but I knew his problem. I knew what he was doing, but no one else at the table suspected.

The second couple was now negotiating with Dong. They had a worse time of it since they wanted soup. The chanting now began slightly louder and faster; "Sliced chicken sandwich, sliced chicken sandwich." People at the next table thought he was praying before dinner.

It was now my turn. Purposely, I order a dish so difficult to pronounce I had Dong confused and upset. Dong was in a tizzy, Jerry was in a frenzy, and I was in my glory. The rehearsing became so loud at this point, people from the other side of the restaurant looked over. They thought Jerry was a psycho arguing with himself. Dong now approached Jerry. The practicing stopped. It was show time!

Jerry was sweating. He had the wide-eyed look of a child at his first visit to a dentist. He waited for the inevitable.

Dong looked at Jerry and asked "And what would you like, sir?" in his best diced English."

After a pause of four or five seconds, Jerry took a deep breath, straightened his body, opened his mouth, and in absolutely perfect pronunciation said "Sliced chicken sandwich." A big sigh of relief and a broad grin then appeared on his face.

Dong dutifully wrote down the order, slowly picked his head up from his pad, looked Jerry right in the eye and said in perfect English, "White or rye, mustard or mayo, chips or slaw?"

At first I didn't have the heart to look at Jerry. Finally after ten or fifteen seconds of silence, I looked over and saw a red line forming on his head, spreading slowly from his forehead down to his chin and sweat poured down his face. A strange gurgling sound started in his throat that finally built to a crescendo of explosive proportions in which attempting to say white, got stuck on his tongue and came out "wh..wh..wh.."

I had three choices. First, I could smack him in the back of the head and force it out. Second, I could tell the waiter "white" myself and stop all of his grief, or…I suddenly had to go to the men's room, to think.….

If there was ever pay back to me for anything I had perpetuated to anyone during my life to this point, it came one morning, at a subway station in Queens, New York.

I worked with Suzy at a major New York City bank. She was redheaded, long-legged and extremely attractive. We were both single, yet were just very close friends. On Monday mornings we would compare our love exploits over the weekend. Hers were invariably more exciting.

On this particular Monday she had a juicy one. Over coffee, she explained that she was in a typical New York singles club on Saturday night, and a typical Don Juan type struck up a conversation with her at the bar. He was in love; so much so that a girl came in selling flowers, and he bought the entire basket for Suzy. Not really interested, Suzy got up to escape and lover-boy took her hand and begged, "Don't leave baby, I've got the hots for you." We both had a big laugh out of that line, but she made quite a mistake in sharing it with me.

Every chance I had, in person, at meetings, on the phone, in messages, I managed to torture her with the phrase "Baby, I've got the hots for you." She just took it and waited, knowing her time would come.

Several weeks later, I had to pick up Suzy at a suburban subway station and drive her to a distant branch office of the bank. It was a busy station at a busy intersection in Queens, N.Y. and I passed by in my car and didn't see her. I found a parking spot and walked back to the station entrance.

Just in front of the station I spotted her looking into a store window. She was always distinguishable with her long, bright red hair and bright green coat with a thick black fur collar. Great, I had another chance for a harassment session.

I slowly snuck up behind her, wrapped my arms around her waist, squeezed tightly, and whispered in her ear, "Don't move baby, I've got the hots for you!"

When she quickly turned around, my blood ran icy cold, and my heart started to pound. It wasn't Suzy! The girl began to scream and I decided that I had two choices, try and explain, or run like hell. Since a crowd was already forming, I felt if I attempted to run, some good Samaritans would tackle me, beat me to a pulp, and my picture would be in tomorrow's newspapers.

As I tried to calm her down, I saw a blue uniform in the crowd. Why are they always there when you don't need them? The fuzz had arrived. Before I could say what had happened, I was shuffled into the back of a blue police car in front of the angry mob that probably contained everyone I knew.

I attempted to explain to the two cops in the front seat, while they shook their heads as if they had heard this exact scenario a thousand times before. Then, out of the corner of my eye, I saw red hair, I saw a green coat, it was Suzy. It was the real Suzy. I was saved! I started yelling "There she is, there she is, go get her. She'll tell you."

They shrugged, yet went over and got Suzy, told her my sad story, and brought her over to the car. I was relieved. Now I wouldn't have to go to prison, and date someone named Snake.

Suzy slowly and cautiously walked over to the squad car. She bent over, looked in at me, smiled, and told the cop, "I never saw him before in my life," and then walked away. I just stared, my mouth open and I began daydreaming of my life with Snake.

Just before they shut the door on the car, she did come back and explain. It was too late though, I was already broken hearted I would never meet Snake.

I vowed then and there, my days of practical jokes were over forever, or were they? It's hard to break old habits, even when they almost get you fired.

Ray was my boss. Ray was mellow. That's the worst you could say about him. He was an easygoing, even-tempered, nice guy...until he met me. I would torment Ray with practical jokes until I had him foaming at the mouth. One of the earliest, and worst jokes occurred in early December.

We were visiting an uptown, Manhattan branch of the bank where we both worked. It was lunch time on a rainy, chilly day. I was with two other people waiting for Ray on a second floor mezzanine.

He appeared about noon and proceeded to a walk-in closet to get his raincoat. He went in, he didn't come out. I don't know what came over me, but I slammed the accordion doors closed behind him and held it closed with my foot.

After about fifteen minutes of screaming, cursing and pounding, there was silence, absolute silence. Nothing came from the closet for about five minutes. Was he dead? At that moment a young, brand new trainee teller appeared at the closet. She wanted her coat. Being a gentleman, I stepped aside.

I don't remember how long she was unconscious. I still don't think it was completely my fault. She was probably very nervous from starting her new job that day, and when she opened the door, Ray came charging out holding an umbrella screaming, "I'll kill you." He had the wide-eyed, maniacal look of a mass murderer. It was probably just too much for her.

After we revived her, she resigned and we went to lunch. I swore to Ray no more jokes. I always swore to Ray no more jokes.

Not till another day!

This year, during my holiday shopping, I experienced flashbacks to a darker time. It was a period of my life I suppressed for twenty years, but it now, somehow, has worked its way back into my conscious mind. These were days of torment, conflict and fear, memories that brought back images of terrible acts of terror, atrocities and torment. These were the years I had worked at.......a discount department store.

I still cringe at the recollections of standing by a table full of handbags while my boss announced on the public address system "*And now on sale in our ladies handbag department, assorted handbags for one dollar each.*" I knew then, what the Marines must have felt like during the Tet Offensive; five thousand Viet Cong storming out of bushes, trees and underbrush with maniacal smiles on their faces, screaming obscenities, running directly towards them with a single motive. These women attacked much the same way. I never saw them coming.

These were also times, I confess, of cowardice. I once abandoned my post in the face of danger. That fateful morning I was at the store's front door, standing behind a cart containing ladies hosiery on sale for nineteen cents. The sale was advertised in the evening's newspaper, and the women were already massing at the front door at six A.M. waiting for the store to open. By eight forty five it was a near riot. Bodies were pressed against the doors being pushed from behind by the new arrivals who every minute swelled their ranks. All of them were just piling up, staring at me, alone behind my cart. At the nine o'clock bell, I knew the doors were swinging open but I just couldn't take the pressure. I cracked and ran for cover in a third floor stockroom. I showed fear in the heat of battle. I never learned how many of my comrades were lost that day.

There were also those visits from the high command to the battlefront.

Once a month on a Saturday morning, the owner of the chain would come to give us a pep talk. He was an elderly man suffering from losses of sight, hearing and some mental acuity, but the store's management still catered to his every whim and wish as he had a reputation for immediate retribution for any disobedience. This particular Saturday he was venting his usual fire and brimstone, when he noticed across the main floor by the elevators, a clerk not paying him any mind and just standing there. A great one for exemplifying the punishment for laziness, he loudly directed the manager, in his thick European accent, "Fire that one over there; the one daydreaming on my time." He then went back to his sermonizing never noticing the manager and his assistant carrying away the offending clerk. The offending clerk happened to be a mannequin who was just doing her job.

My tenure, however, ended in a blaze of glory. I had reached a point in my career where the senior buyers displayed a level of confidence in my performance. Their confidence proved to be both my undoing, and theirs. I was permitted to select and buy from the manufacturer, a collection of ladies house dresses and robes from a catalogue the buyers had sent me. This was indeed a great day in the retail life of a former stock boy. Carefully I pondered the catalogue, spending hours studying and selecting, finally making the call. I ordered one-hundred of this style, two-hundred of this one, totaling about two-thousand pieces in all.

Somewhere in New York the house dresses I had ordered twenty years ago are still hanging on a rack, silently waiting for a buyer. Who knew the manufacturer only accepted orders "by the gross?" The next day the trucks were rolling in, and I was rolled out.

I even tried my hand at horse racing. One would think someone with the charmed life I have lived would do anything to stay away from gambling. Just getting up in the morning was gambling with my life, but to try it with money was really tempting disaster. And it most certainly did.

Having gone to the racetrack on numerous occasions with my friend Louie, who was really a gambler and basically knew what he was doing, I now considered myself quite the expert on horseflesh, notwithstanding the fact, and I didn't always win.

On one vacation trip with a friend to San Juan, Puerto Rico my expertise was really put to the test. After checking into our hotel, we headed directly to El Commandante Race Track. I had my companion, Rich thoroughly convinced we would pay for the vacation, and have money to spare, from our racetrack winnings. So off we went to make our *withdrawal* from the racetrack.

As we were leaving the hotel, I tried to communicate with the doorman while waiting for a cab.

"We're going to the racetrack", I joked. "Any tips?"

He leaned forward and whispered "La Chenga, a sure thing." As any good handicapper would, I stored this information away for future reference.

In the cab, I proudly told the driver, "El Commandant, please."

He looked us over, took us for big players, I'm sure, and whispered "La Chenga, a sure thing." This was getting interesting! We arrived at the track.

A racetrack is a racetrack, anywhere. Drop someone blindfolded in this turmoil of betting windows, drink concessions, and grassy track with the regular cast of characters, it could be any track anywhere in the world. As we walked in, the familiar smell of stale beer and cigar smoke greeted our nostrils. I immediately started guiding my friend through this maze of intriguing activities and strange people. After all, I was an expert.

We finally found our way to the Skyroom restaurant that overlooked the track. Private betting windows for the patrons, tuxedo attired waiters, china dishes, a very classy way to spend a day at the racetrack, but we were worth it, as we were going to win today. I was an expert! After some discreet tipping, we were seated right up front directly at the large glass windows, with an excellent view of the finish line. It was all well worth it. The winnings would pay for it.

We sat, ordered drinks, and perused the area. Our waiter Raul, came over, smiled, leaned over and quietly whispered into my ear, reminiscent of a brokerage commercial, "La Chenga, a sure thing." This was now getting interesting. I had to see this horse! I thought it mat also be good to buy a program.

I raced out to the lobby and pounced on a program vendor. I was able to get the last one. As I walked back to our table, I read the entries for the first race. I scanned down the page and my heart stopped, my head started pounding and my stomach tightened. There he was, number four, La Chenga. This was going to be an interesting day.

As I continued to review the program, I realized they put the record holder for each racing category on the top page of each race. This race was one and a half miles, and guess who was the record holder; La Chenga. I looked up at the odds board expecting to see low, low odds on this champion. Everyone here must know good horseflesh. I knew, because I had thoroughly researched this animal, but what about the others? HE WAS 40-1. My God, I was in the Land of the Morons. I want to move here; I was going to make a fortune today.

Between Rich and myself, we gathered together two hundred and fifty dollars. This was our vacation stake. This was our money for food, casinos and women. Women-what would we be giving up? I hesitated for an instant, and then the sounds of the doorman, cabdriver and waiter kept echoing through my head, "A sure thing." I took the money and walked defiantly to the $50 betting windows. I had a winner. I had a tip. I was an expert.

The ticket vendor never looked up. All I saw was the top of his greasy head. I didn't get a chance to give him my knowing smile.

"Number four; five times please," I said in a voice which in my head sounded booming, but when it came out my mouth sounded like a twelve year old amidst all of these gauchos.

He boringly punched the correct buttons; the machine clicked, whirred and spit out our tickets. I looked at them for a second, sitting there. These weren't pieces of cardboard anymore. They were a new car, new clothes, and girls; lots of girls. I picked the tickets up, put them into my pocket, made a mental note where the cashiers were and went back to our table.

I bought us two large expensive cigars, ordered two steak sandwiches, two of the finest imported beers and we waited. The fact that we had a total of twelve dollars in our pockets meant nothing. We would be flush in the next ten minutes.

The trumpet sounded, the horses pranced out onto the track. They paraded up and down the stretch in front of the crowds. I was worried people would see just how good number four looked, bet him and lower the odds. We were in luck. The odds went UP to 45-1.

I watched La Chenga trot up and down. He looked good. He looked ready. We were ready.

As they entered the starting gate, I wondered if, to save time, one of us should stand at the cashier's window. I decided it would probably be fun to watch the race with the common folk. No rush, we would probably be here all afternoon anyway.

The bell rang, my teeth clenched and the horses leaped from the gate.

The announcer shrieked "That's La Chenga by 10 lengths," my heart raced. "That's La Chenga by 20 lengths," I was sorry I had not wired home for more money. "That's La Chenga by 30 lengths" What denomination bills should I ask for?

I decided I had better get to the cashier. As I turned to leave I took one more look. He was thirty lengths ahead and entering the stretch. He ran out of view behind a long length of high shrubs. The other horses now entered the stretch and went out of view. I watched the finish line for him sauntering to his win. Suddenly number nine crosses over the line. I, of course, must have missed him. I watched the line for him to come back. Meanwhile, number three finishes, as does number four, number seven, number two, and all of the other horses. Where the hell was La Chenga? I stood there in disbelief. I couldn't face Rich until I knew. He sat there with a glazed look. He didn't take pressure as well as I did. I threw up. After apologizing to the man in front of me, I raced down to the finish line, I had to know what happened.

Still clutching my tickets, I ran to the rail in time to see a familiar looking, brown body, being dragged into a truck. The # 4 was fluttering in the breeze.

I learned many things that day;

- I learned La Chenga had a heart attack and died five feet from the finish line.
- I learned he was thirteen years old. They race them in Puerto Rico till they drop.
- I learned Rich was a closet psychotic and could kill if provoked.
- I knew all of this. I was an expert.

When I returned from San Juan I was depressed, broke, and in no mood to make decisions. So, of course, a notice was waiting for me; I was on jury duty.

When the subpoena came I had mixed emotions. It was nice to get a couple of days off from work, but jury duty is basically boring. It's more waiting around than anything exciting. I had been on jury duty in New York City, but now I was living in a rural New York community and knew it would be somewhat different, but different was an understatement.

Bright and early on the designated Monday morning, I headed to the courthouse with a nice letter from my employer asking that I be excused. I thought it would be no problem since it was budget time at the major accounting firm where I was employed and I thought the judge would be sympathetic and say, "That's O.K. Charley, come back anytime."

So here I sat in the courtroom waiting for the judge to make his appearance. I was confident I would be out and back to work by noon. I had a letter.

After about an hour the side door to the courtroom flew open, and two guards led a manacled, shackled, grizzly, wild-eyed young guy into the courtroom. Long scraggly hair and beard, dirty disheveled clothes, I wondered what heinous crime he had committed. I would have liked to serve on his jury, as he was the scourge of society I had always dreamed of sending "up the river." But, I would be gone soon, I had a letter.

They led him over to the side of the courtroom where I was sitting. Actually, they led him into the row I was sitting. Actually, they put him next to me, and handcuffed him to the bench's arm. We just sat and stared at each other.

I was trying to figure out why they would put this obvious felon, in with the jury.

Possibly they wanted us to *mingle*; to get to know him, so we could judge him more fairly. Possibly, it was law in this town that murderers get an even shot at killing the jury, before the trial. I just didn't know. We just sat and stared at each other.

At that point, they started calling names to break us up into various juries for upcoming trials. One by one, they called off names, filling row after row with groups of twelve, numbering Juror one, Juror two, etc.

They were about to call off Juror four, when I was listening intently for my name. "Jerome Tibbs," the Judge called. No one moved. "Jerome Tibbs," he called again. The convict next to me stood up and shuffled out to the aisle. He moved to the row in front of me. "Charles Barron", the Judge called. Dazed, I stood up, and once again they put me next to Charley Manson, but this time one row up. He continued to call off names, and completely fill up the row.

I had to know. I squeezed past Crazy Jerome, and went over to the bailiff and asked, "What's with Buffalo Bill. What did he do?"

The bailiff looked at me, smiled and said, "Right now son, he's the foreman of your jury. The Judge has been trying to get him in here from the hills, for over three years. He's not leaving here till he's finished with jury duty. Since he was picked first, he's your foreman. You work for him, right now," he smiled and walked away.

I immediately went up to the judge and gave him my letter. It was time to go. He read it, smiled, ripped it into hundreds of little pieces and gave it back to me.

I looked back over at my row, and noticed that my *associate* was now trying to chew off his steel handcuffs. I sat back down, and decided right then and there, that however the *boss* votes, I agree.

4.

PLANNING A WEDDING-
THE HOLY WARS

For the most part, the first 30 years of my life, although riddled with personal disaster and misfortune, does not compare with the sheer turbulence which began after my marriage. The stories related henceforth were always recounted for amusing conversation at dinner parties and the like, but the universal comment has always been directed at my wife Karen, "How do you put up with him?" It is a question neither she nor I could ever answer. What quality in this woman allowed her to share the dark cloud, the twin accommodations in hell house, and the banishment to Charley's World? Just how did I seduce this lamb to the slaughter? Actually, you can blame my mother for that!

It was about to happen again. Every unmarried, Jewish male's nightmare: the blind date. Between the ages of 17 to 60, if you are single, you are fair prey for every aunt, cousin, mother or friend who is ready, willing, able, and eager to "fix you up." The girl is always the nicest, most pleasant, smartest girl you have ever met, with the best personality you could imagine.

Since Moses led the wandering tribes, this immortal tradition has been passed on from grandmother to mother. It was even suspected that Abraham's mother carved into a stone and had delivered to him the message "Call me, have I got a girl for you!"

And so, here we were again. Almost twenty years ago to the day. A phone number presented to me by my mother within the framework of an ancient Hebraic ritual; coming silently into my room while I lay there watching Gilligan's Island; placing the paper upon my brow she spoke the centuries old Talmudic chant "Call her. She's a nice girl. Are you afraid you may like her?" Also true

39

to scripture, I usually disposed of the names and numbers in a manner consistent with tradition, into the sacred wastebasket.

As the police have their confidential sources that never seem to dry up, so do Jewish mothers. It always amazed me that she could come up with three or four new numbers a month. Sometimes I wondered if there were actually only two girls just changing their names and phone numbers around to confuse us. However, this time it was different. I actually held on to it. This time I actually called it. I don't know why. Was I was getting older? Was I getting smarter? Was she just wearing me down as Nazi interrogators wore down their prisoners during the war?

When I told her I was calling this one, tears welled up in her eyes and she immediately sat down and started making up the guest list. "Don't book the hall just yet," I cautioned. Yet, as I was dialing the telephone, she was looking through a book of invitation samples. To say she was hopeful would be an understatement.

I did call, and I did take out for the first time one of *Mom's picks*. Bear in mind, my mother had no firsthand knowledge of this woman. All data was secondhand from, supposedly, reliable sources.

Returning from a surprisingly enjoyable date, I found her waiting up for me looking particularly hopeful. "Well, how was it? Was the restaurant good? Was the movie nice?" She was avoiding the obvious question she was dying to ask. Finally, after ten minutes of verbal sparring with her, she could take it no more. She shrieked, "So, how was the girl? Was she nice? Was she pretty? Will you ask her out again? Talk, tell me." After receiving affirmative answers to her questions, she was relieved and, now, even more optimistic. As she walked to her room, I called to her once more, "Hey Mom, you forgot to ask one question."

Turning she smiled and asked, "What's that?"

"You didn't ask me if she was Jewish." She just laughed and walked into her bedroom confident that her source of supply knew her requirements.

Someday in Queens, New York they will find the body of the well intentioned matchmaker who just got her wires crossed once too often and now lies in a shallow grave. Someday they'll track down the crazed mother who gave here son one phone number too many. For the date, was red headed, fair skinned, and very Irish Catholic and I married her. So much for tradition!

Now when I say "I married her," this is a simplistic summation of six months of a process which is only exceeded in its complexity and danger only by the construction of an atomic bomb. Planning a wedding, even under the most ideal conditions, is stressful to say the least. The delicate operation of bringing together a Jewish and Catholic family for a wedding makes the Palestinian peace talks a walk in the park. The first time I even broached the topic, the results were surprising to say the least.

Driving home from an evening at a friend's home, I finally had enough courage to ask; "Why don't we get married?"

"Pull over", she begged, "I think I'm going to vomit." That was the last we spoke of it that night. Later, I lay in my bed wondering if we were still dating.

We went out two or three more times without any more discussion of the matter. One evening, we were watching television, when out of the blue, she asked, "If we do decide to get married, when would we do it?"

"Right after the ceremony, I understand there's a room at the catering hall where you wait before the reception. We could lock the door."

"I meant, moron, when would you want to have the ceremony?"

"Oh that," my excitement had calmed down to practicality. "We would have to work that out with the caterers. I think you have to give them about a year."

"A year!" I heard myself saying. Could my hormones hold out for that long? That's an awful lot of cold showers.

"I guess we could do that," she finally answered. She did have terms. First; the kids would have to be raised Catholic, which I had no problem with, being a closet Jew, and second; that she required naps every Saturday and Sunday afternoons, for the rest of our lives. This I treated as a political promise, and said yes, but had absolutely no intention or interest in abiding by it after consummation of the marriage.

So there we were, engaged. Far from the typical movie version of a proposal, but at least she wasn't throwing up. The next major challenge; breaking it to the families.

My mother took it surprisingly well. I had anticipated her excusing herself from the room and taking an overdose of Mah Jong tiles, but actually she was relatively calm. We didn't find out until later that she knew she had terminal cancer. Since I was already 30, she probably thought I was gay and was relieved to find out I was marrying a Catholic as opposed to someone named Gary.

Telling Karen's family wasn't as traumatic as I had anticipated. In a previous *encounter,* she had given her family a worse case scenario, which made this union at least less obnoxious as it might have been.

Karen's former boyfriend was also Jewish, but fanatic enough to run off and join the Israeli Army. Karen's parents would, I'm sure, rather visit their daughter and Jewish son-in-law in Queens, New York, rather than have to crawl under a barb wire fence on the West Bank.

The next phase in this military style operation was the 'first dinner' between the families.

Initially, the two armed camps, sitting on opposite sides of the table, just stared at each other. It must have been very similar to the Camp David Peace Talks. I understand there was also some discussion as to the shape of the table, but since Karen's mother only had one table, this became a non-issue.

As for the menu, pot roast, ham, potatoes, Kasha (Jewish Rice), Christian Brothers and Mogen David wines, apple pie, apple strudel, it was like a gastronomical United Nations. The freeze finally lifted, and all were talking and laughing. Then someone raised the issue of seeing the caterer.

Caterer's have the unique ability to make you feel whatever you've ordered, isn't enough. It is their job to "sell the big party." They know much better than you, what you want. After all, they have been doing it longer!

Karen and I were sitting across from Jeffrey, "Call me Jake," Rosenfield. He was booking agent for one of the largest caterers in Nassau County, New York.

"And how many do you think will be attending, Mr. Barron?

"Not more than a hundred. We're trying to keep it small.

"I'll tell you exactly what will happen", Jake lectured. "You'll invite 150 to be sure of 100 coming and 135 will show up. You would had told me 110, and we'll be short and people will be sitting on the floor eating their filet mignon. Trust me. I've been doing this for twenty five years. Tell me 125 and be safe."

"What happens if only 90 show up?" I asked

"Oh, you would still have to pay for 125. We already cooked for that many," was his answer.

"You have, what looks to be, a very comfortable floor. Write down 100," I directed.

This is not going to be easy I thought to myself.

"Now", he said rubbing his hands together, "the food."

By the time we were finished we had a cocktail hour with five hot dishes, twenty cold salads, and three roving waiters with appetizers. There were three stationery bars and two rolling ones. The dinner consisted of prime rib with all the accouterments. And for desert, he talked us into what's called a Viennese Table. Simply stated, it is every desert ever concocted, conceived, or imagined and then some. There were enough things on there to feed a small country for several months.

"And now as to the ceremony, will you be using our chapel?"

"Among others," I answered.

He looked confused and I explained further, "We're going to have an afternoon performance at a church and the evening performance, a Jewish service, here."

He started rubbing his hands again, "Of course, you want us to provide some refreshment at the church after the first service?"

"No, No, that won't be necessary. The Catholic guests are tough, don't need food. The communion wafer will keep them fine until dinner. It's the Jewish group we have to feed and kept fed. No stamina!" I had just about enough of this guy. If we stay any longer, he'll offer to cater the consummation in the hotel room.

Over the next few months we saw a parade of men and woman who knew exactly what would make our wedding, "An affair to remember" My idea of "An affair to remember" is Kathleen Turner drugged and tied up, on a remote desert island. This was going to be a wedding, a necessary evil to document to the world you are legally married, before sex.

Photographers to "Preserve forever this magic day;" musicians to "Make your wedding come alive;" florists to "Add beauty and color;" tailors to "Glamorously clothe the bride in the finest silk and linen;" chauffeurs to "Elegantly transport you and your bride in a stretch magic carpet;" and the men of the cloth, Rabbi and Priest,"Perform the sacred rites to join you in the eyes of God." It just went on and on, everyone with their hands out and their mouths going, selling you everything from bouquets to salvation. This production had more producers than Gone With The Wind.

Since we were going on a cruise for our honeymoon, we decided to test our seaworthiness. What better place for this than the Circle Line, a three hour sightseeing cruise around the island of Manhattan, New York. To fully appreciate this story, you must know that Karen is meticulous in body and home, shy, and although not a teetotaler, an occasional glass of wine is the limit.

The big mistake we made, which set the tone for the rest of the day, was the fact that we brought only twenty dollars with us. Not nearly enough; fifteen dollars for the cruise, two fifty to park, and a buck twenty five for tolls. This left us with a dollar twenty five to blow on having a good time.

It was 105 degrees on the outside deck, not a breath of air, not a seat to be had inside, where it's air conditioned and we were dressed in our worst. By the end of the day we looked like merchant seamen on the Titanic. We were hot, dirty, soaking wet, tired, hungry, thirsty and seasick. A wonderful afternoon on the water, and we had a buck and a quarter to recover with.

We decided, on the way home, to stop off at our favorite Chinese restaurant and order out. We didn't think they would allow us to sit in their chairs in our current condition. We talked of sitting in the shower at Karen's house while we ate. The food was no problem, they took credit cards, but something to drink was the challenge since the bar needed cash. We had enough money for one drink.

We ordered one ice-cold Budweiser. I can't remember before or after this day, of Karen ever drinking a beer. When it came we just looked at it for a minute or two, and, since being a gentleman comes second to death by thirst, I grabbed the bottle and quickly downed my half while Karen watched, her dry parched lips screaming, "Please hurry."

As Karen grabbed for the beer, she held it close to her chest as to protect it from the highwaymen. Meanwhile, they called my order, which I picked up and left, assuming Karen would follow. She didn't. Karen was too engrossed in her beer to see me leave.

Returning to find her, I stood at the door, across the restaurant and watched. There she stood, nervously taking sips of beer, while alternately keeping it protected to her breast. She thought I was still there, so she was chattering away. She was dirty, wet, sand covered with hair strewn in all directions, and talking animatedly to the air. As I watched, people near her at the bar, started moving away for fear she would go on a killer rampage at any moment.

When she realized what was happening, she put the beer down, and petrified with shame, raced out of the bar. The bartender feeling bad for this vagrant, took the beer and chased after her outside of the bar and up the street, to return it to her. What a sight!

To this day, she will not go back to this restaurant for fear after years they would still recognize her as "The bag lady".

Now being engaged, we had to start thinking about furniture. Did we do it the easy way and go to a neighborhood store? Nah! What is the point of that. That's the simple way and nothing unusual may happen. We had to be different. We had to go "out of town for the furniture."

Vermont is a beautiful state. As we drove, huge green mountains suddenly loomed over the road, while lush forests and small quaint towns alternately lined the highway It was summer, yet I could envision the hustle and bustle, when wintry snows turn these sleepy neighborhoods into a skiing Mecca. We were on our way to Rutland, a focal point in season, but now a quiet, picturesque village. Karen, her brother Jesse, her sister Mary, and I had decided on a quick trip for furniture hunting and a short vacation.

As we pulled into the driveway of a bed and breakfast that had been recommended to us, three large, black Doberman Pincers came ambling up. They weren't growling or acting hostile, but saliva running out of each corner of their mouths was enough to freeze me in my seat. Shortly, a young woman appeared, introduced herself as Ann, the owner of the Inn, and ordered the dogs to the back. She apologized and told us that they were actually friendly, but they do keep the bears away at night.

"Great!" I thought to myself. "Everything I love, big dogs and bears. What a great weekend this will be, if I live through it."

Ann showed us around the house, which turned out to be quite beautiful with oak paneled rooms and antique furniture throughout. She gave Jesse and me the front bedroom, with Karen and Mary, in another room directly in back of ours, with a large connecting door. Ours was actually a sitting room for theirs, but it was fine since both rooms were extremely large with big double beds in each.

We spent the day in town, browsing at various furniture stores and sightseeing. After dinner at a local restaurant, we headed back to the house as a strong thunderstorm was brewing. After returning, we decided it was time for bed. It was now after ten and we wanted to get an early start the following morning. As planned, Karen and Mary took the back bedroom, and I shared the double bed with Jesse.

After we turned out the lights, I realized just how dark it could get in the country. Living in the city all my life, I was not used to a complete lack of any light whatsoever. It was difficult to fall asleep, pitch black and graveyard still, but after about an hour, I was out cold.

Thinking back, I was never really sure what first woke me up, but about midnight, the storm was really in full force. The thunder came in waves, clapping and shaking the house, while torrential rain and hail pummeled the roof and windows. Lightning sparked so brightly, it looked as if the room was being bathed in strobe light. Off in the background, barely perceptible, was a low, yet deep moaning sound, interspersed with the billowing thunder. Briefly, I thought of waking Karen or Jesse just to hear it, but I felt silly, as it was just probably the storm. I just lay there and listened.

The storm grew in intensity. Lightning was flashing every few seconds in tandem rhythm with the crashing thunder. The moaning was now distinctively developing into an audible growling, becoming louder and more voracious by the minute. Lightning, thunder, pounding rain and hail, alternating with vicious growling; it was like being in a Stephen King movie.

As I formulated my escape plans, I knew intellectually that there was a perfectly reasonable explanation for the situation I was in, but I speculated that it was probably caused by one of three things;

a) The Dobermans, we had encountered earlier, had somehow gotten into the house, and if they locate me, they will probably rip me to shreds.

b) A bear, we had heard about earlier, had somehow gotten into the house, and if he locates me, he will probably rip me to shreds.

c) Having seen "The Exorcist" the week before, I knew what a demon sounded like, and if he located me he would possess me, and together we would rip everyone else to shreds.

Although the last alternative was definitely preferable, it was by no means acceptable, so I decided some action was called for. The growling was now much more pronounced and guttural. It was getting so loud that now Karen, sleeping in the next room, was awakened and started shouting to me.

"Charlie, is everything all right?" I was too petrified to respond.

She continued calling, "Is everything okay out there?"

I stayed silent. My reasoning was that if I answered, it would zero in and get me. If Karen kept calling, it would find her more easily, and be so satisfied after destroying and eating her, it would just leave. I loved Karen, but these were desperate times.

I was now thinking about leaping out the window to go for help when I noticed that another sound was now appearing to alternate with the growling. Had it brought a friend? Indistinguishable at first, I started recognizing words. Immediately I abandoned my Doberman and bear theories, and concentrated on the demonic possession possibility.

After several minutes, the voice was becoming recognizable and somewhat familiar. In a flash of lightening it came to me. To prove my suspicion, I hauled off and smacked Jesse in the back of the head. He ricocheted off the wall and bounced back into bed, now wide awake. I wasn't finished. I started beating him around the head and shoulders for all the grief he had caused me. I was ready to abandon my beloved to an unknown force, because of his snoring.

After it quieted down and everyone was again asleep, I just watched as Jesse started up his incantations once more. I still wasn't fully convinced my third theory was altogether wrong and wished I had some holy water to sprinkle on him just to be absolutely sure. But then again, I'm Jewish and the water probably wouldn't work.

As the countdown proceeded, why would I think everything would go well? One evening about three weeks before the wedding I was at Karen's home and started to feel ill.

It was now 11:00 P.M. By 1:30 A.M., I had come up for air from inside the sink once. My insides were coming up through the top of my head. "Call the doctor. I'll be dead by daybreak." I guess she finally agreed this was for real. Karen called the doctor.

"Bring him in to the hospital. I'll expect their call after they examine him."

My Doctor has spoken! God forbid he should get out of bed, and actually go to the hospital when it's dark outside. I'd always wondered if he was night-blind.

I was in pain, I was nauseous, I was dizzy, I was vomiting, Karen was driving fifteen miles an hour and stopping at every red light. If she was an ambulance driver, the morgues would be standing room only.

The hospital we were heading to was not a metropolitan medical center, but a small, suburban hospital established by physicians who couldn't get affiliated with other hospitals, for one reason or another.

As a matter of fact, when we got to the Emergency Room, the door was locked. We had to ring the bell and a nurse asked us through a peephole who had sent us, then let us in. It was very similar to what I always imagined speak-easy would be like. This did not impart to me great feelings of confidence.

At this point I was doubled over with pain and I could hardly walk. No wheelchair, no help, no compassion. The nurse and Karen walked ten feet in front of me as if I wasn't even there. If I had fallen down unconscious, no one would have ever known.

We eventually got to an admissions desk, where I sat down in a nearby chair, thinking I could tell the admissions clerk the information. This was not the case. Hospital policy required, that the patient fill out the form themselves. *I wonder what they do when the patient is unconscious.* The desk was about five feet high and again, Karen was nowhere to be found. I think she and the nurse were having coffee somewhere.

Finally, I saw a doctor. He walked in, pushed my belly down with his entire weight, heard me scream louder than I have ever screamed before, told me I needed an appendectomy and walked out. Dr. Schweitzer he wasn't.

Within thirty minutes, I was shaved, and not my face, then wheeled into an operating room. The first one I had ever been in and it was just like in the movies. A huge bulbous light overhead, tables full of shiny instruments, masked nurses *(in this hospital it was probably to cover their identity)*, oxygen tanks, and all overshadowed by the bright, stark white walls.

On the left side of the table, the anesthesiologist had my arm flat on a board with various tubes running out of it. The surgeon sauntered over to the table, picked up a scalpel, paused, and then raised it over my midsection. I motion to the anesthesiologist. He leaned over, put his ear to my mouth, as I screamed, "Does he know I'm still awake?!"

After everyone stopped laughing, I felt a burning in my arm and I was out. I woke up in a room, sore and tired. I had tubes in my arms, tubes in my nose, tubes in places I can't even mention. They had yanked out my appendix supposedly minutes before it burst. *Karen probably had 5 or 10 minutes more she could have waited at that railroad crossing.*

They told me I would be in the hospital one week, which left two weeks to heal quickly for my honeymoon.

I called Karen when I woke up. It was a little after 5:00 A.M. and I hoped she was home. For all I knew she was out for breakfast with the nurse.

My first disappointment was that the phone rang seven or eight times before she picked it up. I thought she'd be waiting by the phone, grabbing it on the first ring with pointed anticipation waiting for news of my condition.

"Karen, it's me. I'm still alive!"

"What time is it?" she sleepily said.

"Karen, I'm all right. I'm alive. We can get married in two weeks, make wild, wet love and stay in bed for two weeks till you're so sore you can't walk."

"Who is this?"

"Can I speak to Karen please?" I asked her mother.

"Hello," a groggy voice got on the phone.

"Who is that?" I still heard her mother asking.

"Who is this?" Karen was now asking, as if she was expecting seven or eight calls at 5:00 A.M. of persons reporting their medical condition to her.

I gave up and went to sleep.

True to form, I was in the hospital up to three days before the wedding. The hospital stay was uneventful aside from Karen trying to shave me with a straight razor and losing it beneath the bedcovers. That would have been consistent with the Barron curse, appearing at my wedding sans one useless organ and one very much desired one. The big day did eventually arrive and I was ready!

5

HONEYMOON IN JAIL-ALMOST

The morning of the wedding, I was at the doctor's office bright and early. He checked the stitches, gave me a massive shot of B-12, patted me on the head and said I would be fine.

Now I was then off to the hotel we would use for the first night before leaving for our honeymoon.. I checked in, brought over the baggage, tested the bed for resiliency, and left.

I looked great in my tuxedo. No one could tell I had about thirty stitches across my belly which ached as I walked. We met with the bandleader just before the reception to clue him in. "Ringo, you have to remember, don't call us up to do any strenuous dances together like the Hora, a very exerting Jewish dance. I'm in pain, I have stitches, I could bleed to death. DO NOT CALL ME UP TO DANCE!"

"No problem'. No dancing, got it."

"And now, introducing them for the first time as husband and wife, Mr. and Mrs. Charles Barron'" Ringo screamed into the microphone to the drum roll. As we walked in, he shrieked, "Charles and Karen will now lead everyone in the traditional Jewish dance, the Hora."

I was about to run for my table when six people grabbed us, formed a circle, and pulled me in all directions, all over the dance floor. I cursed Ringo as I was dragged and twirled, spun and pushed.

Finally, I was able to break free and get to my table. I was about to sit down, when the accursed photographer came by. "A group picture," he screamed.

It is a photographer's sworn duty to take a minimum of 6,000 proofs at a wedding to be sure that you buy at least 100. As I stood there behind the dais with the wedding party, I started to feel dizzy from all the dancing. The next thing I knew, people were loosening my collar and throwing water in my face as I lie prone behind the table. To this day, we have the picture he had taken at the moment of my falling, showing me conspicuously missing.

Another try at a group picture, with Karen's parents behind us, and all holding champagne, led to someone supposedly hitting her mother's arm, dousing me with her glass of champagne. Her uncle, a priest, ran over and tried to baptize me, then and there. *They never gave up.*

People ate, people drank, people danced, and the chopped liver and ham spread flowed. Soon the music died down, the crowd disappeared, and were we alone in our hotel room, on the bed looking at each other.

Unfortunately, my sister, Paula, was also there sitting on the bed between us, making up a list of guests and their gifts for future reference when reciprocity was necessary. *Her patented 'S—list'.* She made appropriate comments and notations whenever she thought the gift was adequate.

Eventually, she left, and we were really alone to begin our rocky life together, after a very rocky beginning.

The next morning we were on a plane heading for Miami and our honeymoon cruise. Five days and four nights of lounging on a ship, doing absolutely nothing but eating, sleeping and whatever else people on honeymoons do. I stared out the plane's window as the engines droned comfortably on. The wedding went fairly well, considering the fact I had just been released from the hospital after an emergency appendectomy. The preceding days were hectic at best, but I was now going to make it up to my bride, my new wife, Karen. A nice quiet trip.

The plane landed, we collected our luggage, *four large suitcases of which underwear and a toothbrush were mine,* jumped in a cab, and headed for the first stop in our 'Deluxe Honeymoon Package,' a night at a famous Miami Beach Hotel. The driver dropped us at the curb, and Karen and I struggled with all this luggage into the lobby. I still had stitches in me and a doorman was nowhere to be found.

I left her in the middle of the huge lobby with this vinyl mountain and went to check in to our "Spacious Honeymoon Suite, where you will enjoy comfort and privacy," as the ad had described. After giving the desk clerk my name, he came back with a somber look. I was expecting, "Yes sir, here's your key," but instead I heard,

"We have a problem. We tried to reach you."

"Did you try the hospital? That's where I've been for two weeks," my head was screaming, but instead I calmly said, "Really, what is it?"

"Your tour company went bankrupt. The voucher and registration you have are no good. We thought you knew and we gave your room away."

"Are there any other rooms?" I managed to gasp, looking over at Karen, sitting, smiling, waving, confidently at me in the middle of the lobby with most of our possessions.

"No sir, a convention in town took most of them, I'm sorry."

I had to tell her. I thought she may become suspicious if we slept on a couch in the lobby. I explained the situation, and she just gave me a blank stare as if saying, "O.K., my father would know what to do....fix it." I had to do something.

I went back to the desk and did what I do best; I begged. "Isn't there anything you can do? We just got married, and I recently had major surgery.

I don't know how long I have left. Please!" I thought I was getting to him. He mused for a minute and finally said, "Wait a minute, I'll talk to the manager. Do you want to sit down?"

"I'll be all right for a while. My wife has to give me my pain killer shot soon, though. Do you think we can use your office?"

"I'll be rrright back," he stuttered and left.

He was back in five minutes with good news. A small staff room was available that they would let us have complimentary because of all the trouble. Things were looking up, or were they?

Small was the key word here. There was barely enough space in the room for us and the luggage, let alone trying to open the pull-out bed. In order to open it, Karen had to hold two of the bags up over her head against the wall, while I struggled with the bed. I couldn't pull too hard or lift too much because of the stitches, so Karen held the bags up with one hand and helped me pull out the bed with her foot.

After we finally got it open, the bags collapsed down over Karen, flinging her into the bed. All she could manage to say was, "These things never happened when I traveled with my father."

We made it through the night, packed, and got out to the street. We could board the ship at 9 A.M., and I couldn't wait. As I looked out the cab window, I just fantasized about our "Luxurious Stateroom with full amenities, where good times will abound," as the brochure described. As we pulled into the Port of Miami, the driver asked me what berth the ship was in. I had memorized it, as the tickets were all I had to read all night.

"Berth #22," I proudly told him.

We were passing all the other beautiful cruise ships. Berth 12; there was a nice one; berth 17, 18, I counted as ship after ship flashed by.

"Here's #22 Sir," the cabby announced.

We looked out to see this magnificent vessel. Water, all I saw was blue-green water, lapping up against a deserted pier. My heart sank.

I left Karen on the dock with the luggage, and ran inside the terminal to find out what happened. It was about 110 degrees outside, and it was a relief to go into an air conditioned building, no matter how crowded it was, and it was.

Wall-to-wall people were lining up at the various cruise companies represented. I finally found our company and got in line behind about twenty five people.

Forty-five minutes later, I reached the front and asked the clerk incredulously, "Where's my ship?"

After checking his records, he said those all too familiar words: "We have a problem. We tried to reach you, but we couldn't. Your ship broke down at sea. We had to cancel the trip."

"I just had major surgery," I went into my well-rehearsed speech ending with, "and this could be my last cruise ever."

He hesitated a moment, winked and said, "Give me about a half-hour. I'll see what I can do."

I had to tell Karen. I didn't want to tell her because I knew if I told her I would hear the 'father' story again, but what could I do? She knew a ship was supposed to be there; she saw a ship wasn't there; she would only stay out there on the dock so long.

I walked outside to the dock area and a blast of hot air hit me. She'd been out here for the last hour and she was not going to be very happy. As I walked over, I noticed that Karen and her luggage were surrounded by ten or twelve dock-workers, sitting on orange crates, just talking and passing around a large bottle of wine, each taking swigs. It looked like an Indian pow-wow. There was my bride, sitting on one piece of luggage with the other three suitcases circled around her like covered wagons. With her purse huddled to her chest, Karen bent over, soaked with sweat, refusing the bottle every time it reached her, and I'm sure thinking, "Why me?"

Here I was, cool and dry, and when she spotted me, I swear she actually growled, "Where the hell have you been? The guys and I have been wondering."

I explained the best I could and told her I had to go back in. She just gave me an icy stare, sat back down, and as I turned to go back, screamed, "Hey, let's have that bottle back here."

When I got up to the front of the line again, the cruise manager was smiling. He held an envelope containing the new tickets and told me, "I've put you on one. It leaves in ten minutes, Berth 5. No change in price, we'll eat the difference." I grabbed the tickets, thanked him, and raced out to Karen. He was shouting something behind me, but I knew all I needed to know. My main purpose now was to get on that ship.

I didn't even explain. I just screamed, "Let's go," grabbed one of the bags, gave her three, and ran screaming at her, "Come on, come on, they're not that heavy."

We raced up the pier being cheered by Karen's new drinking buddies. As we charged up the gangplank, Karen just stopped and said, "I can't make it, go on without me." I figured a honeymoon without the bride was lacking, so I grabbed another bag and we finally got on board.

We found the room, which turned out to be a suite, and finally sat down on the bed and rested. Catching her breath, she innocently asked, "Where does this boat go to?"

Those words echoed through my head like a cannon going off next to my ear. I had absolutely no idea where we were going. I had left so quickly, I had forgotten to ask. As I confessed my ignorance, a faint smile appeared on her face.

I thought she was finally seeing the humor in all of this. Crossing her legs, she asked very officiously, "I know this is a long shot, but by some chance, would you have any idea whatsoever, how long we will be gone?" I just sat there, staring at her, afraid to say, "Not an idea in hell."

She started laughing. Not a happy, infectious laugh, but rather the maniacal kind you hear in a horror movie just before a knife comes flying out of the air into the hero's back. She continued laughing, walking slowly into the bathroom where she stayed most of the morning. I just sat there in the room, thumbing through the tickets, trying to figure out how to tell her we were in the wrong room.

Then the honeymoon actually started going downhill, if you can believe that.

Our cruise eventually took us to the Bahamas, and the duty-free shops of Freeport. Since we had gone wild and purchased everything in sight, I knew there would be trouble at the border. The heinous customs agents would be waiting. The only hope I had was to lie, but what about my new wife? Could she stand the pressure? When Karen and I were dating, I came to understand the difficulty she had in telling lies. Now, twenty years later, she has perfected this skill to an art form, but then, she did have a problem.

The solution, I felt, was to be prepared. We began to rehearse. I was the big, bad customs agent and she was the passenger.

"Do you have anything to declare?" I would ask.

"Nothing to declare," was all she had to say. "Nothing to declare!"

We practiced for days, back and forth until she had it down perfectly. The return trip had changed from a honeymoon to a mission. A mission to stiff the government. We practiced until the big day came!

As I remember, it was a bright, sunny day when we pulled back into the Port of Miami. I was ready; she was ready; we were ready. His name was Bob, the customs agent. I know that because he said it five or six times. It was his first day on the job, and he wanted to catch someone.

He wanted a Colombian drug dealer, a Libyan terrorist, anyone. He wanted action, and here we stood in front of Bob, who was looking for a big bust. But we were ready, we had rehearsed. Those twenty hours of "nothing to declare" would pay off now.

I put the bags on Bob's counter and stared him straight in the eye. I looked at my wife, gave her a knowing smile, and waited for the big question. We were ready!

It was probably my fault. I should have noticed it, but I didn't. A small bead of perspiration was forming over her left eyebrow, a slight twitch in her right eye. I should have been watching her but I was too confident.

Bob looked me over, smiled, and then began to speak. Karen's right hand began to tremble slightly.

"Do you have anything to declare?" he asked.

It was anticlimactic. I had sounded more menacing than him during our rehearsals. I was about to answer when I looked over at Karen. Sweat was pouring down her face as if she had just walked out of a sauna. Her eyes had the glazed wildness of a frightened stallion, and she was breathing erratically.

Before I could say my part, she screamed out "He made me do it! He made me lie!"

Bob leaped into action. He thought he had hit the mother lode. With one hand on his gun, he signaled for reinforcements while moving my wife away from me. "Move away from her real slow," he said with almost a John Wayne inflection. He thought I was holding her hostage.

They took me into a little room (*reserved, I'm sure for major drug smugglers*), and they had me empty all my bags and pockets onto a table. All in all, after two and a half hours of searching and questions, the ordeal cost me $540 and my dignity.

Karen's only explanation was that Bob was good. She couldn't take his questioning. She folded like a cheap camera. My only consolation was that Bob never brought out his rubber finger.

Did the fun stop there? Did we have enough sense to call it a day and come home at that point? Need I say more?

The second leg of our honeymoon took us to Florida and Disneyworld. We arrived at our Orlando hotel late in the day, yet I still had hopes of seeing the Kennedy Space Center, as we had a full schedule the next day. It was a two hour drive and they closed in two and a half hours. The solution was simple, speed.

I was traveling at about ninety miles per hour on the Beeline Expressway headed to the Space Center when Karen, casually looking out the window, asked me innocently, "There's a policeman on the side of the road pointing a machine at the car. What does that mean?"

"It means I'll be getting a ticket very soon, Karen," I said as the flashing red light appeared in my rear view mirror.

I pulled over and waited. Eventually, the Officer sauntered over. I don't know if he had a fight with his wife, or what the problem was, but he was in a bad mood. He immediately started yelling and lecturing me on the evils of speeding. Karen, becoming highly incensed at his attitude, decided to write down his badge number and opened the glove compartment to rummage through and look for a pen. He did not take kindly to this.

He must have thought she was going for her Uzi. All of a sudden, I felt cold steel on my cheek. I looked over, and found myself staring into the barrel of a very large gun pressed against my nose.

"Don't move son," he cautioned. A thought immediately crossed my mind. He thinks SHE is going for a gun, and he's holding a gun, to MY head. What's was the point?

"Don't shoot, lady or I'll blow HIS head off," I imagined him saying. I always thought, maybe naively, that you pointed the gun at the person holding another gun at you, not some innocent bystander, on the slim hope that the gunman would have some concern about the passersby's safety. Considering what had happened over the last few days, boy was he wrong. I was worried at this point Karen had fleeting thoughts of an empty seat on the plane for the trip home.

Karen continued looking for the paper and pen.

"Karen", I begged, "He's going to kill me".

"That's O.K. I have his badge number. He'll be in big trouble.", Karen yelled.

"Karen", I tried to speak slowly and reason, "He'll kill both of us and take the paper. Please close the glove compartment".

Eventually, she agreed and did.

He made me get out, put my hands on the side of the car and frisked me, just as in the movies, except this time it was me, and it was for real. I was being intimate with an irate cop, while my new wife was in the car, hoping I am sure, that he finds something and she could go home alone.

After assuring himself we weren't Bonnie and Clyde, he gave me a ticket and another lecture on not making unexpected movements while being lectured by an officer and let us go. He never even looked at Karen. We continued on our way, and by far, the Space Center was not the most exciting aspect of that day.

6

MARRIED TO CHARLEY-
A DANGEROUS JOB

The early days of our new life together proved that marriage did not minimize the powers of the evil curse I was under. Somewhere, sometime, an ancestor must have obviously insulted a wizard or gypsy as the curse was still potent. Only now, my new wife Karen was included in its web.

Being a good husband and having the day off, I volunteered to pick up Karen at the subway station rather than her suffering the long bus ride home.

Queens Boulevard in New York, as most subway stations, is a madhouse at rush hour with no parking spaces to be had. I decided to wait around the corner and was forced to double-park. Possibly I had the radio on too loud, possibly I didn't, but I just sat and listened to the music.

About ten minutes into my waiting, the car I was blocking wanted to leave, so I pulled out and raced around the block anticipating pulling into the now available space.

As I pulled around the final corner, I saw someone who looked strangely familiar. She looked like Karen, yet she had a torn dress, one missing shoe, and was bleeding from both knees and both hands. The first thing I thought of was that she had been mugged in the subway. I leaped out of the car barely letting it stop, and ran to my beloved's aid.

I was met with a left uppercut to my throat and a barrage of curses any long-shoreman would have been proud to know. During a second rabbit punch to my kidneys, I was able to ascertain that just before I had pulled out, she snuck up to the passenger side of the car, put her hand into the door handle, and when I abruptly left, she was caught, hanging there and dragged around the corner, until hitting a fire pump which snapped her free from the door handle.

All I can say is she should have made more noise!

My sharing of the Barron curse with Karen was in no way limited to the ground, sometimes we took it to 30,000 feet.

Karen is afraid of flying. This is an undeniable fact. The entire time she is on an airplane, she is petrified. If I fall asleep, she wakes me up, so I can take over the shift and she could sleep. If one of us weren't listening to the engines, they would shut off.

On this particular flight returning to New York from New Orleans, where she had joined me on a business trip, we were landing at Kennedy airport. Landing at Kennedy Airport at night, is particularly unnerving for the squeamish, since many times you approach over Jamaica Bay, and it is pitch black. You have no prospective of land or altitude. On this flight I sat by the window and was just staring out into the blackness upon our descent into Kennedy. She was half asleep since I was on duty, and just as a joke, I said in a low voice, *"I think we are going to ditch"*. A big mistake…

She woke with a start and repeated my statement, but loudly for all to hear, "WE'RE GOING TO DITCH!" Immediately, I heard the passengers directly in front of us scream, "We're going to ditch!" Like a wave at a baseball game, it went up to the front of the plane, and down the other side, until behind me a male passenger leaned over and told me, "We're doomed."

Luckily, at that moment we landed. I raced off the plane through empty aisles since the other passengers were still dazed by their close brush with death. I wanted to be off before they could trace the source of this rumor.

Karen, whom I had left behind, told me that as people filed off, they were congratulating the pilot for his saving the plane.

I'm sure he was both gratified and extremely confused.

Sometimes I torment Karen on the ground, but at airports. I'm an equal opportunity tormentor. I discriminate against no location.

Years ago I had decided never to fly on one of those deep discount, no frills airlines. I wanted the frills. I wanted a life jacket under the seat and a rubber raft in the back. I wanted pilots who were old enough to shave and stewardesses who weren't. I wanted my warm coke and cold meal and I wanted a vomit bag. What I didn't want were planes with happy faces painted on their noses and pilots who took tickets before takeoff and sold sandwiches in the aisle afterwards.

But now, I was married and I had responsibilities. Since and we were off to see Karen's sister in Milwaukee, a trip I really did not want to take anyway, now was the perfect time to try one of those 'no-frills' airlines. I was sure the rest of the trip would be 'no-frills' also.

We were able to buy a thirty nine dollar round trip ticket between New York and Milwaukee which worried me. How could they do that? The fuel for the trip alone must cost fifty dollars per passenger. I had a lot to learn.

We were flying *Peoples Express*. For the uninitiated, *Peoples Express* was the first of the 'no frills' breed. Now defunct, for good reason, it was a leader in giving you more of less than any other carrier in existence at that time.

They considered reserved seats and checked luggage 'luxuries,' which added a new dimension to flying.

We had never flown this type of carrier before and thought the $200 per ticket difference was worth not having a hot meal. Boy, were we wrong! I dropped Karen and our five pieces of luggage off at the terminal and put the car in long term parking. I had the only piece of carry-on luggage with me. As I placed it into the x-ray machine I was congratulating myself with the precision of the trip up to this point when all of a sudden, bells went off.

In retrospect it wasn't really smart to pack the five piece knife set we were bringing as a gift into a carry on bag. "You can't bring knives onto the plane," lectured one of *People's Express* finest. "We will check this for you, free."

"Fine," I embarrassingly conceded, I guess one glitch in a trip, I could handle, but what does he mean free? When I finally reached Karen, she informed me that checking luggage is a 'frill.' Unless we pay three dollars and fifty cents per bag, we would have to try and squeeze our five large suitcases into one of those overhead compartments. We paid and checked them in, but upon seeing the size of the seats on the plane, we would have been better off putting the luggage in the seats and climbing into the overheads ourselves.

"What seats do we have," I naively asked Karen.

"They told me it's first come, first serve when you get on the plane," Karen told me. "First come, first serve?" I really didn't understand what this entailed until I saw the other passengers massing at the gate. Since under Karen's engine alert schedule we had to sit together, we joined the mob and stood ready for the assault.

Until the time the gates swung open, I had no appreciation of what it was like during the gold rush-land giveaway days of old. Men with attaches, woman with shopping bags, children, people with canes and in walkers, all running as a mob helter skelter towards the plane. I led the pack for a while, neck in neck with a man being pushed in a wheelchair, with Karen back amidst the mob. "Save yourself", she was shouting, with I yelling to her, "Don't look back, you can do it." And we did. Of course, since I was in the plane a good 3 minutes before she came flying in the door propelled with the crowd, I had to lay out over two seats feigning not understanding English, while other passengers beat me around the face and neck for the seats.

The actual flight was more like a baseball game than an airline trip. Every few minutes, people were in the aisle hawking various products such as cokes, beer, souvenirs, magazines, emergency evacuation instructions and sandwiches. The sandwiches could actually be used as flotation devices in the event of a water landing.

The return trip began much as the first. I dropped Karen and the luggage off while I returned the rental car. I still held my one carry on bag, and once again bells began to ring at the trusty x-ray machine.

"What's that?" asked the airline's representative pointing to a grid-like silhouette on the screen. While in Milwaukee, we had purchased a trivet, which is a grill top with legs, upon which one places hot pots and dishes. It was too easy to just tell the man this, so instead I opened my big mouth and confessed, "It's just a small Hibachi. Since you don't serve food on the plane, my wife and I decided to grill some hot dogs and hamburgers and sell them to the passengers."

"You can't do that!" shrieked the rocket scientist I was now dealing with. "No, No, No, you cannot do that," he continued his ranting, now drawing a crowd.

Just then Karen appeared. "What's going on," she asked.

I walked over to her and told her, "That man, (pointing to Einstein) would like to speak to you." As she approached him, I faded into the crowd and walked over to the gate.

"My husband said you wanted to speak to me. That is my bag you are holding."

He just jumped right in to his oratory, "You CANNOT barbecue hot dogs and hamburgers on a plane. It is dangerous and in violation of FAA regulations."

Karen, now taken completely by surprise agreed, "That's a very good law, I agree 100%."

"Ma'am, do you understand, you cannot sell any hot dogs, hamburgers or cook anything of any kind on the aircraft?"

"Charleeeeee," I barely heard her screams as I walked to the gate just thinking to myself, "I really miss my frills......".

Even after all of the incidents to date, Karen still trusted me to some extent. She still had a modicum of faith that there must be some areas that I knew what I was doing within. After this next adventure, I really sealed my fate.

One morning upon waking, we discovered it was raining. We wanted something to do. In my distant memory, I remembered some correlation between fishing and rain. I knew rain was a benefit to fisherman, yet I was foggy as to just how. I have since learned the relationship is, that it was good to fish AFTER a storm. At that time I remembered it as fishing DURING a storm......

So off we went! It was Hurricane David as I remember, and Jones' Beach was the place. Decked out in our fishing gear; new, bright yellow rain slickers, large round, bright yellow Nor'easter hats, a bag of fat bloodworms and rod & reel, we were set. We made ourselves comfortable on a double-decker dock on a pier at the beach while rain and fifty m.p.h. winds lashed out at us. We were the only ones at the beach, yet she still had faith. She asked me only once, if I was positive of my facts. I reassured her. I told her to trust me. All was well...we began to fish.

As the wind forced the rain onto the dock where we stood, the decking below our feet began to disappear into the murky puddles in which we were standing. I placed our precious bag of bait worms on the main pier above and behind us, and thought about retreating to a higher elevation ourselves.

Trying to enjoy the scenery, I looked around at the dark green water pounding the beach, the ever darkening sky and the vanishing dock below us. We were alone except for a sole seagull which had walked by us four or five times on the dock above. I thought he was being friendly. Little did I know he was actually casing us for the kill.

About five minutes later, the wind was really starting to whip up. I was trying to decide if we should lash our bodies to the railing, when out of the corner of my eye I spotted movement at the far end of the pier. My friend, the seagull, was racing full speed down the dock towards us, reminiscent of a 747 taking off. He picked up my bag of worms in his beak and continued his escape running erratically down the pier.

This was the last straw. I'd been mugged by an errant seagull on a lonely beach while fishing in a hurricane. Neither the police nor any of the tabloids would believe this story.

I decided I must seek vengeance myself. I picked up the closest thing, a new fishing knife, took a deep breath, let out my finest Rambo attack scream and proceeded to chase this winged devil up the dock.

Karen, sitting quietly with her line still in the water, knee deep in ocean, holding on with one hand to the railing, rain pelting her wide brimmed hat, looked up and turned to the commotion. She saw me chasing this bird up the dock into the fifty mile per hour gusts, knife in hand, shouting obscenities. She got up, slowly packed up the gear and dejectedly walked to the car.

It was time to go home........

Sometimes I was the recipient of the whammy, but it really wasn't my fault. Karen had become the expediter of doom and helped me embarrass myself.

It was raining. Not just a normal heavy rain, it was the dampening kind of dark, chilling, thick, rain that soaks you to your soul. That's the only reason I decided to wear a raincoat that morning. I usually never wear coats, but on this morning I needed one. I was heading downtown on business and it would be wet.

I dug out the only raincoat I owned from deep in the closet. It was gray, double breasted, old, and I immediately noticed it had no buttons. No buttons! I now had to do something I avoided whenever possible. I had to do something I rued and which was so distasteful to me I started to get sick to my stomach. I had to ask my wife Karen to sew.

She had other good qualities: A good cook, smart, attractive, but put a needle and thread in her hand and it's Helen Keller at the controls of a 747, Mickey Rooney on the Knicks, or Willy Sutton as a bank teller. It was an act against nature and nature always got even. But, I was desperate.

She was as surprised at my asking as I was. It had been almost five years since the last incident. She has sewn her boss' sleeve to his chest before a big dinner he had to go to, and the newspaper account had stated that at first he thought he was having a stroke and couldn't lift his arm. I had no other choice. It was now time for her newest venture into seamstress hell.

I paced while she sewed. She sewed while I paced. I was late and it felt as if it had taken forever. Finally, all eight buttons were back on, and I grabbed the coat and ran.

It wasn't until I was downtown coming out of the subway that I put the coat on. I don't remember how old it was, but it was at least, three sizes too small. It was now raining so hard that I squeezed into it anyway and tried to close the buttons, as the wind and rain buffeted me. What a surprise, she had sewed each button at least three inches higher than the hole to which it belonged. Here I stood, waiting at the corner of Madison Avenue and 53rd street, New York City, stuffed into a coat which was cutting off circulation to my aorta and at the same time, because of the off-center buttons, contorted my body into a shape which should only feel comfortable swinging from a bell tower.

As I huddled there in the torrent, hunched and pinched, wet and blown, a passerby walked over and handed me a one dollar bill. She thought I was a handicapped, homeless, street person. At first, I was surprised. The shock then turned to laughter, then to practicality. How much, I wondered, could I collect if I stayed here all day? As I fantasized, my associate showed up and we went to the office.

I spent the dollar on coffee for the two of us.

Sometimes we even tried to tempt the fates by doing something intellectual. The results were always the same, but with 'style.'

Karen likes the opera. She had always liked the opera. When we had first met, she had given me tickets to *La Traviata* for my birthday and I suffered through it. Agony it was, but I liked her, and in those days I would do anything if I had a shot at sex.

Now, we were married and she wanted to go to the opera again. I agreed as I was still trying for sex, but this time I wanted to share the misery. I invited everyone I knew, but wound up with only eight friends coming, including my déclassé, best friend, Jerry. So there we were, headed for "*Carmen.*"

In order to not make the evening a total bust, we decided to go for Chinese food first. Karen hates Chinese food, but she, realizing what a sacrifice I was making, acquiesced. Actually, she was still in shock that to this point that I hadn't found some excuse not to go.

I enjoyed the meal. I enjoyed it despite the fact I had Chinese food for lunch and dinner every day for the last two weeks. I was working near Chinatown and took advantage of the location.

We arrived at the theater and I sat next to Jerry, who was as happy with me for dragging him here, as I was with Karen for the same reason. People in colorful costumes ran off and on the stage singing their hearts out. Large men with deep voices and thick bosomed women with high, shrill voices, all took their turns. Jerry and I just sat and stared. For some reason, my left arm and leg were getting numb, but I just ascribed this to boredom.

It was the big parade scene and things picked up for a while. Dozens of people marching, accompanied by horses prancing out in tune to the music, subtly followed by costumed men with shovels. As if coming out of a trance, all of a sudden, Jerry bellowed out "If those god-damned horses start to sing, I'm getting the hell out of here." The section of the audience surrounding us broke out in hysterics.

I started to feel dizzy and now my face was feeling numb. I knew something was wrong when I began to dribble. I could see, I could hear, but I couldn't move or speak. My face was numb and the left side was paralyzed and saliva was drooling out.

Karen looked over at me and matter-of-factly said, "Stop it, we're not leaving." Then she turned back to the show, ignoring me completely. I thought I was having a stroke, she thought I was faking.

They finally took me to the hospital, when twenty minutes after the show ended; I was still sitting there drooling.

The diagnosis was Bells Palsy, monosodium glutamate overdose. The doctor sarcastically asked me if I was mainlining it. I said, "No, just too much Egg Foo Young."

Even at home relaxing in a simple bath becomes a major event and embarrassment.

Saturday night is bath night, everyone knows that. So there I was, relaxing in a hot tub, filled with some of Karen's bubble bath, playing with one of my toy boats.

Tiring of the boat after a few minutes, and not seeing any other toys nearby, I was bored. I started counting wall tiles and scraping some mildew from cracks. I made music by rubbing my arms against the sides of the tub. I caught drops of water coming out of the faucet with my big toe. I plugged up the faucet with my big toe. I jammed my big toe into the faucet. I was stuck.

I accidentally had inserted the big toe of my right foot too deeply into the faucet and I was wedged tight. No matter what I did, I could not remove it.

Of course, consistent with my luck, no one was home and Karen wasn't due back for two or three hours. This could be a very long bath.

There I sat, feeling like a complete moron, water ice cold after two hours, shriveling up into a prune-like creature, toe still stuck in the faucet, when I hear a key in the door.

"KAREN", I shrieked. "I'm stuck. Get me out of here."

The bathroom door flies open, and there stands Karen, two female neighbors, whom Karen had invited back for coffee, and two of their kids, all gawking at me. I tried to remain calm.

"Karen, I could use some help please. The first thing is, COULD YOU CLEAR THE ROOM?"

Amidst shrieks of laughter, Karen ushered the women out of the room, came back, sat down on the edge of the tub.

"What's new?" she sarcastically smirked. "What a lovely shade of blue you're turning. Can we run down to the paint store, that's exactly what I've been looking for?"

"Get me out of here now. This water is freezing." I was in no mood for games.

"By the way, any reason why you didn't flip up the drain with your foot and let the water out? Just a thought."

I just stared at her.

Finally, she starting pulling at my leg. No luck. "Sit on it," I screamed in desperation.

Now you have to picture this in your mind's eye. I'm stark naked in the tub, She stripped down to underwear, so as not to get wet, sat on my leg facing away, and jumped up and down as if riding a horse. The pressure now on my leg, caused a sharp, searing pain in my foot and toe, and I let out a loud scream. The neighbors, sitting in the living room came running in, took one look, said, "Oh, my God. Excuse us!" and ran home.

At that point, she refused to help me anymore and said she would call a plumber. I begged her to try one more thing.

"Karen, turn the water on as high as it will go. The pressure will force out my toe."

"O.K. Last try," she warned me.

With that, she turned the faucet as far as it would go. I felt pressure on my toe, and expecting it to fly out of the faucet, braced myself. All of a sudden, I heard a loud whoosh and was being showered with ice-cold water. The entire pipe, holding the faucet, came flying out of the wall, with water spraying out uncontrollably. My toe was still stuck, and the pipe was still attached on one end.

"Call a plumber! Call a plumber!" I kept screaming.

I was in agony. Trapped in an ice cold shower with nowhere to go. Karen, finally feeling sorry for me, gave me a raincoat and umbrella. It was an incredible sight.

When the plumber finally arrived, he really didn't say too much. After staring for a minute or two, he just said, "I've seen toes in faucets. I've seen pulled pipes, but this, this is one to tell the boys at the shop."

He fixed it, got my toe out, took his check and left. Never asked how, never asked why. But I'd bet the ranch, that night at the bar, he had some story to tell.

7

SOMETIMES I DO IT TO MYSELF

The doctor's final prognosis was that I'll live but I would need to go on a diet. I had just finished a diet. In fact, I had just finished my twelfth diet this year. They all work for a while, then the diet becomes the problem instead of the solution.

Take, for example, Slim-Fast. It's not a bad meal, a nice chocolate malt for lunch without the guilt of a real shake. After a month or two though, it became boring, and I wanted more. You would be amazed just how good a Slim-Fast shake is with two scoops of Hagen-Daz vanilla in it.

Nutri-systems is terrific, also. They have exceptional stuffed cabbage. After three or four portions at dinner you're really stuffed. A nice Slim-Fast float would really finish off such a meal.

Weight Watchers was great, too. Eat anything you want and just mark off those little boxes. When you run out of boxes, you're finished eating for the day. By the time I dropped out, I had eaten through July 12, 2006.

A diet is for the mind, not the body. It gives the comforting illusion that you are doing something worthwhile for yourself. There is only one reason most people go on diets. The underlying motive for the agony, pain and suffering one puts themselves through during this ritualistic torture usually aren't health, religious or spiritual. It's not psychological, social or humanistic. It is triggered by one of the most traumatic experience's one can endure. It is something that has or will happen to everyone: rich man, poor man, beggar man, thief. Sometime, somewhere, everyone sees themselves naked in a full length magnifying mirror. It is indeed a shattering experience!

Once it happens, you can never be the same. It's like hearing your voice for the first time on a tape recorder. It seems strange, foreign. Who is that mass of flesh with my head on it? It must be one of those carnival mirrors. It's Candid Camera. Then after you realize that this is really the way you look sans clothes, you reach the next level that is anger. But strangely, you're not angry at yourself. You're furious with the Papa John's, Ben & Jerry, the Colonel and the Pillsbury Doughboy. You immediately hate the owner of your favorite Italian restaurant, the French for their fries and the Wise potato chip owl. Basically it's everyone's fault but your own. Next comes acceptance and the desire to immediately start a diet....tomorrow.

And so it happened to me. As the groundhog on that famous day, I saw something that really scared me. But instead of going into my hole, I went to a diet doctor. For the uninitiated, this is a physician who specializes in making people thin. He weighed about 350 pounds. This exuded little confidence in me when I first met him.

After our initial discussion and a physical, he told me I was overweight and should really be on a diet. This man should get the Nobel prize for medicine. I'm 5'8", I weigh 220 pounds and he spots right away the fact that I need a diet. Perhaps he just never saw himself in a mirror.

He put me on a low-fat diet. This made sense to me, if you eat fat, you get fat. Logical, decisive, I was getting my confidence back. I could eat up to twenty grams of fat per day. This sounded reasonable since twenty grams seems like an awful lot of fat to be eating anyway. This was, until I looked at the label of my favorite breakfast sausage that had fifteen grams of fat per sausage or my favorite frozen lasagna at twenty one grams per slice. That's all right, I'll just stick to vegetables.

I swear to you, I stayed away from fats. I had no bacon, ham, beef or ice cream. I ate no Chinese, Italian, French or pastrami. For weeks my lunches were Mexican. But instead of all of those nasty, fattening tacos, enchiladas and fajitas, I had vegetables. Nice lettuce covered with guacamole, black olives, cheese and sour cream. For dinner a platter of creamed spinach, creamed corn, more guacamole and a salad. Snacks were sunflower seeds or peanuts. Breakfast was a peanut butter sandwich on light toast. I gained ten pounds in two weeks.

"Didn't you look up the foods in that fat content guide I gave you?" asked my bloated mentor.

I really thought fatty foods looked greasy. I thought they had to be crispy, fried and oily. The portly practitioner said on my new low fat diet, I was probably eating about 150 grams of fat a day.

Perhaps I'll try exercise instead!

8

FRIENDS & FAMILY-NO ONE IS SAFE

It may seem to the casual observer that the storm clouds I live under only affect my life with my immediate family. This is, by far, not the case as one will see by the following examples that involve extended family and friends alike. I am an equal opportunity nemesis. Even my best friend Jerry was not immune to the Barron scourge.

After fishing once or twice I considered myself quite the expert. I then decided I should be a disciple for fishing. I had to spread the word. Who else should I convert to this great hobby but Jerry, my best friend. We had, of course, to go out and buy him some gear.

He trusted me. *Everyone trusts me the first time around.* I instructed Jerry, "You've got to buy the best. You'll catch more. The fish know." He went for it hook, line & sinker, with the best rod and reel at $375.00.

Off we went to the wilderness I had conquered just the week before, Jones Beach New York. It was spring this time. "Sissy weather for fishing," I thought, but what the heck! I led the troops to my special place. I set up Jerry's line and then my own. The men fished; the women talked.

I don't know what made me nervous when Jerry cast. He was a big boy, so when he pulled his rod back and with a mighty stroke forced it forward, I should have expected a long cast. Was it the five ounce sinker I had put on his line? Was it the three minnows on his hook? Something was not right.

We watched as his line unraveled as if a Great White Shark was hooked. With a high pitched squeal, the tackle raced into the shy as if shot out of a gun. We watched as it kept going and going and going.......

It just kept going. I had forgotten to tie the end of the line to the reel. It just went.

As we stood watching his line float away, I suggested that Jerry try and catch the end with the tip of his rod. He ran into the water, reached as far as he could, and dropped his rod. It floated out, racing the line for open seas.

He looked at me and I thought I was next. At that point he remembered his wife. He must tell her. She was not particularly understanding about money. She was tight.

We found his wife on the beach with our bucket of minnows, throwing them back into the ocean singing Born Free.

It was time to go home....

My sister Paula also managed to tread into my zone of terror on several occasions.

Paula was getting married and a big affair was to be held. After months of planning, the day arrived.

The tuxedo my future brother-in-law had chosen for the ushers to wear must have been hard to find; brown velvet jackets with thick, black satin collars. The only reason I mention the wardrobe is that it had a direct bearing on the trouble I had gotten myself into. In fact, it is what lawyers call 'a contributing factor.'

The reception was held at Leonard's of Great Neck, which is a landmark for weddings in the New York area. A huge gothic mansion with twenty reception halls, Leonard's is a veritable party factory. They had it all down to a science. Ornate lobbies with massive chandeliers, thick carpeting, pandering maitre d's and 10 brides running around at any one time. It was a sight to behold, and there I was, all decked out in my rented disaster. I was so flashy that people kept asking me which band I was with. But it was time to party.

I was never really a very good dancer, nor did I ever enjoy dancing. So in order for me to get down, I had to be somewhat 'in my cups.' For the less polite, I had to be somewhat inebriated. I knew since this was my sister's wedding, I had to be at my peak form since I would be called into action by assorted aunts, cousins, and sisters. I decided some preparation was in order. The cocktail hour was just before the ceremony, which just preceded the reception, so it was now or never. I mingled and drank. I drank and mingled. I was beginning to feel like dancing.

At that moment, halfway through the cocktail hour, someone told me the wedding party was to assemble in one of the basement photo studios for group pictures. In my present condition, I was ready for dancing, not walking. I would have to find my way down there myself which was not an easy task.

After several tries, I managed to find the basement. Not really used to drinking heavily, I was feeling very happy. I could barely see. I roamed around this complex of photo studios, brides, cameras, and lights. I finally zeroed in on the brown velvet uniform the rest of my flock was wearing.

"I have arrived for pictures," I announced. No one looked up, no one really cared. Since I am somewhat older than my sister and her fiancé, I knew very few of their friends, or for that matter, his family.

They just put me in line, told me to smile, and off they went into snapshot land. I just stood and smiled. Wherever they pushed me, wherever they pulled me, I just smiled. I was still so happy, I couldn't even see the camera, but I'm sure there was one!

About forty five minutes later, it was almost over. I was still smiling, but now I was starting to sober up and I could see more clearly. As the group disbanded, I was able to get a good look at the happy couple now posing alone. How beautiful she looked, how handsome he was. His hair perfectly combed, his shoes perfectly shined, his beard perfectly trimmed. But wait, the future brother-in-law I knew had no beard. The sister I had grown up with was a brunette, yet this bride was blonde. To my complete and utter shock, it appeared I had taken wedding pictures for forty five minutes with the wrong wedding party.

As I tried to fade into the crowd, I felt a hand grip my shoulder. I thought I was busted. I started to turn around and heard a familiar voice, "Where have you been? We've been waiting for you." It was my sister. My real, flesh and blood, brunette sister. Quickly, I escaped to the correct studio, and once again, I smiled.

Sometimes on cold winter nights, as I sit staring out the window into the deep darkness, I think of a happy couple. A happy couple married almost twenty years ago. A pretty, blond girl and a bearded man sitting night after night thumbing through their wedding album asking each other, "Who is this man?"

Paula has been a key player in many of these episodes. Paula & Billy have the unique ability to take common everyday tasks and do them with a unique twist.

The first time Karen & I had Thanksgiving dinner at their home, she set 'the bed' and all ten of us knelt on the sides and ate off the mattress. The motif was Japanese/PosturePedic. The explanation was no table large enough.

Once when Billy lost a filling, he Super Glued it back in. Don't even try and imagine what he does when he finds hair in the sink.

Paula landed a job at a local supermarket as the 'Drake's Duck' giving out pastry samples. It was obvious she took her job too seriously when she started calling her baby daughter "her quisling" and wore the duck outfit on errands to the bank and the like. It was also then she decided she needed an above ground swimming pool.

As nutty as Paula is most of the time, it is I who am the star player and onto whom the universe seems to cave. There was one time though that her husband Billy seemed to go off the deep end, but alas since I was there, it was probably my magnetic aura that did him in.

Paula and Billy decided to rent a truck and move themselves from their apartment to a house they had bought not far away. Since they had helped us on our various occasions, of course, we were obligated to help them.

We parked the kids at my in-laws, and showed up at her house bright and early at 7:00 A.M. Paula, of course, was still asleep. Billy had gone to pick up the truck, so we waited with other assorted relatives and friends in the street. After all, Paula needed her sleep.

Billy returned and we started moving out the furniture. It was strange, but I didn't see any of the traditional masses of cartons one sees during the course of a house move. Actually, as we soon found out, we didn't see them because they weren't there. She had not packed up yet. This move was going to be 'Au Natu'ral'; no boxes. I believe a French mover invented it. It causes less trauma on the books, dishes and glassware.

We moved a china closet with the china still in it (very delicate.) We moved a bookcase with the books still in it (very heavy.) And we moved a bed, still made, with Paula in it (very strange.)

When Billy's Uncle Peter and I picked up the bed, underneath were dishes neatly stacked, comics and magazines piled high, and books of family photos, still loose.

Peter looked at me and asked, "Did anyone tell Paula she was moving today?"

We packed, shoved, stuffed and crammed. We threw, pitched, rolled and piled, all the furniture, pictures, toys, dishes, towels, and everything else that was loose into one twenty eight foot truck. If it had been packed, it probably would have taken an eighteen footer, but loose stuff needs more room to move around, I guess.

Closing the doors to the truck was like stuffing an over packed suitcase closed. We barely made it. I really didn't want to be around for the grand opening, but I guess I had to see it through.

We were in front of the new house waiting for Billy with the truck to arrive. Suddenly, around the corner, a long yellow truck appeared. Karen, I, and the rest of the crew all stood there watching. It was like a kid waiting for the school bus. You're relieved to see it, but really don't want to get on.

He stopped and got out. We all stood there and looked at this long, yellow monster gleaming in the afternoon sun. Such an innocuous looking thing, yet it contained horrors like Pandora's Box. Open the door, you didn't know what you would be releasing.

Someone had to be the first. I approached with caution to the side door, slowly opened the latch, and eased the massive door open, just a crack. I tried to look inside. All I really saw was the backs of some pieces of furniture. It looked reasonably safe. They were standing upright and not moving.

I took a deep breath, yanked open the door and said a short prayer. A false sense of security settled over me. I was about to climb up into the truck when I looked up into a mountain of books, toys, and collectibles, showering down on me like an avalanche. I was on the ground buried in bric-a-brac. What a terrible way to go, covered in knickknacks. My life flashed in front of me with images of winding up, stuffed, on a table in a flea market.

Karen, as usual, saved me, pulling me from the rubble. I asked for mouth to mouth resuscitation to which, of course, she refused.

One by one, we climbed into the truck to assess the damage. The furniture was intact, but dishes, crystal, books, glassware, anything which normal people usually pack, were strewn with varying degrees of damage around the truck. Some we could unload by hand, some went under the shovel.

We unloaded most of the truck, leaving the beds for last, as they were going upstairs and probably would be the most trouble. It was a very long, hot, nerve-racking day, but the worst was yet to come.

Billy's father grabbed one end of a king sized mattress and I the other and headed in. The staircase to the top level was rather narrow, down at a forty five degree angle from right to left. We tried to negotiate the turn several times to no avail. There was no way these babies were getting upstairs.

Billy came in behind us and saw our problem. He was already at the brink, from all of the other disasters to this point. I think this was the straw that broke the camel's back. He let out a short guttural groan, ran out to his car, and came back with a large ax. He shrieked, ran to the wall behind the staircase, and started hacking away at the plaster. He was chopping out huge chunks of the wall while smirking like Jack Nicholson in the Shining. We all just stood and watched.

"Somebody should do something!" his father said to me.

Looking at the rhythm he was getting with the ax, and the obviously sharp edge to it, I looked at his father. "He's your kid. Maybe he won't chop you to bits."

"Shouldn't we call someone?" he asked again.

"911 would be good!" I answered.

He was down to the beams and couldn't go any further without possible structural damage. Luckily, he stopped.

He threw down the ax, ran outside, and came back with a saw. "He's going for the beams, tackle him," his father screamed.

Instead of the wall, he jumped on top of the mattress and started sawing it down the middle.

"Good idea, Billy," I said quietly, as I started edging towards the door. I wondered what other tools he had in the car. Hopefully, there was no chain saw.

At this point Paula came in and saw what Billy was up to. Expecting a hysterical outburst, I was surprised when she said "Oh, trouble getting it upstairs? You had to cut it?"

"She's crazy too!" his Uncle Frank confided in me.

Eventually, he finished sawing, took it upstairs, and when we all left, there was Billy and Paula, super gluing and sewing, so they could eventually go to sleep.

An interesting day, all in all. The only thought I had on the drive home was that, thank God, Billy wasn't a tailor. Could you imagine what he would do to get someone into a suit?

Sometimes it's not even my fault but I still wind up with a headache as in this little episode when my father-in-law decided to buy a new car.

I am a good negotiator! This reputation is not unearned. A short time ago a Toyota salesman actually asked me to leave during a bargaining session. He said, "I was too intense."

Since this is common knowledge within my wife's family, when my father-in-law, Jim, was buying his first new car, his wife asked me to accompany him. "Get the best price," was my charge. Charley was being called up to active duty.

Jim was too nice a guy. He was like putty in the hands of salesmen. Insurance, appliance, encyclopedia, he couldn't say no, and didn't like to argue. He trusted everyone and did not believe anyone would cheat him. A very foolish set of values to live by in New York City.

We arrived at the dealer and were looking around the lot, when one of those infamous automobile salesmen appeared. He was well dressed, clean-cut, friendly and I hated him on sight. He introduced himself as Raymond and immediately started making small talk with Jim, who seemed to take to him. So much so, that at one point I thought he was going to ask Raymond home to dinner.

Jim explained exactly what he was looking for and, of course, Raymond had exactly that car on the lot. Exactly, except for a couple of dealer-installed options and it was the wrong color. Raymond walked us over to the car. There it stood. A brand new Chevy Nova, light brown, loaded with options. Jim was smiling, Raymond was salivating, and I was worrying.

I whispered to Jim, "Don't smile. It isn't exactly what you want, but you're willing to talk."

"I love it," he screamed to the salesman.

"This is going to be tough," I thought. "I'm fighting both of them."

We went inside to talk. Raymond tried to send me for coffee, but I stuck close to Jim. If I left him alone he might have bought a fleet. Raymond started writing up the estimate, while he was telling us that three other people were interested in this car, so we had better act fast.

Jim leaned over and whispered to me, "We better sign quickly; someone else may get it."

"You're the only one that's getting it, Jim," I thought to myself.

He came up with a price of $11,450. Jim said "Great," and was looking for a pen to sign with. I pinned his arm to his leg and told the salesman.

"We just saw this exact car down the road for $10,200. Why should we buy it here?" Raymond, talking directly to Jim, said "He's low-balling you. He can't really sell it for that price."

Jim started arguing with me. He had forgotten that I had made the whole thing up. "How can he sell it for that price?" I put my hands to my head.

Raymond then said "Look, if you buy today, I'll make it $11,000. I really can't go any lower." Jim screamed, "Fine," as Raymond tried to hand him a pen, which I body blocked with my arm.

"Make it $10,500 and he'll buy," I parried.

Raymond now sadly shrugged to Jim, "I guess we can't do business today."

I motioned to Jim to get up and fake an exit. I was halfway out the door when I spotted Jim leaping for the pen from Raymond's hand.

I raced back just in time to grab the contract and make one last plea. "Make him throw in the radio and mats," I begged Jim. Jim's hand was trembling, signing his name in the air, trying to get closer to the paper.

"OK, OK," relented Raymond. "An A.M. radio and half-mats, but you're killing me." At this point, both Raymond and Jim looked at me with anticipation, awaiting my reply. "Yes," I gestured, "yes." Jim and Raymond shook hands, now relieved they had defeated me, the enemy.

Leaving the dealership, Jim turned to me and confessed, "You know, I really didn't like the color"

Every once in a while, my father-in-law knew better. He knew a 'better' route to get somewhere, a "better" restaurant to go to, a 'better' man to vote for. When he knew 'better,' we argued. Sometimes I won, sometimes I lost, but it always felt 'better' to win. This particular time….I won.

One bright and sunny weekend in July we invited my in-laws to accompany us to a theme park in New Jersey called Great Adventures. Part of the complex was the traditional amusements, but the larger section was called Jungle Habitat, a drive-through safari. Here, from the safety of your car, you were able to see all sort of animal species, dangerous to tame, chimps to rhinoceros, all up close and personal.

When we picked them up, my father-in-law had a 'better' idea. He wanted to drive his spanking new Chevy to the park. Even after I suggested that we go in my older station wagon, as I had heard there was a danger of the animals climbing all over and scratching your car, but he knew 'better.' He said that the animals were afraid of cars and would stay clear. There would be absolutely no danger, whatsoever. After arguing for about an hour, I gave in and, we left in his car with him driving. I had lost, for now.

We arrived at the animal compound and it looked, felt and smelled as if you were in darkest Africa. The illusion was incredible. There were no fences or cages, and your only defense was your car and roving sharpshooters in jeeps, who interceded only in the event of a serious incident. We began to drive in.

He laughed, "Gosh, I hope we come out alive." I just smiled and waited.

We drove in further. A lion lounging in the sun to our left, a peacock prancing by, I was hoping for more. We drove deeper into the Congo. Quiet, serene, birds chirping, what kind of a jungle is this? Suddenly, a small chimpanzee jumped on the hood of the car. We were surprised, but no-one was worried. I was starting to lose hope, when a second, then a third chimp appeared. A small glimmer of worry crossed his face.

"Get off there," he yelled, picking up speed slightly.

Suddenly fifteen to twenty chimps were all over the car, a giraffe was licking the driver's side window, a bear was lying on the hood licking the windshield, while two lions parked themselves right in front of the car. He started to sweat, and I felt 'better.'

We found that honking horns, revving engines and sudden thrusts forward would not budge this menagerie that had all but attached themselves to his car. We stopped and waited for assistance. I was now smiling ear to ear as his car was virtually covered in monkeys, bears and other assorted jungle dwellers.

After we were rescued and were safely out of the jungle, he stopped to scrape off the remnants left by our visitors on his hood. He admitted that perhaps I was right, after all, and we should have taken an older car.

They say all good things come to those that wait; they say patience is a virtue; they also say that truth will triumph. All this may be so, but sometimes a dozen bananas smeared all over the outside of a car, will help success along......

Once in a great while, I am actually asked to perform a task which the requester should have known full well I am incapable of doing without the great potential for chaos and disaster. I bear no responsibility in such cases, especially when the assignment involves fire. All I can say is, she should have known better.

My sister-in-law Mary hates bugs. I mean she doesn't just dislike insects, she is petrified of them. Many a night when we were living nearby, I had to go on a midnight spider run to her house.

I mention the above, to firmly establish the level of misery caused to her by something my pal Jerry and I had inadvertently done.

I guess I use that phrase "inadvertently done" quite a bit, but it is always true. None of the actions reported herein were done purposefully.

One Sunday afternoon, Jerry, his wife, Joyce, Karen, and I were going to visit our townhouse being built in New Jersey. So we decided to drop in on Mary, who lived nearby, to say hello. Karen's mother and father were already there.

"Why don't you and Jerry start a barbecue, and the rest of us will go over and see the house?" Mary suggested. *She lived to regret the statement.*

The barbecue she was talking about was a small Hibachi on her deck. We agreed and they left.

It was clouding up, so we tried to get it going quickly. I found the charcoal, dumped it in, and loaded it up with starter fluid. Jerry threw a match and off it went. For a small Hibachi it produced a very large flame. Leaping yellow, red and blue flames crackled up through the grille. Possibly, there was too much charcoal, maybe it was just a dab more lighter fluid than I needed, but in any event, it was a rip roarin' fire.

The problem the flames created was actually not our fault. Mary had never cleaned out the bottom of the Hibachi. We failed to notice that at least four inches of rainwater had collected on the bottom along with thick grease and grime. Combine this with intense heat, and you don't have to be a forensic chemist to guess what this produced, SMOKE. Thick, black, sticky, billowing, blowing smoke.

One other small miscalculation on our part may have added to the final messy conclusion to this epic. We had forgotten to close the sliding patio glass door or screen door.

We learned an interesting thing about smoke that afternoon. It drives any kind of insect, flying or crawling, out in front of it, from the way it's blowing. By the time we realized this, her apartment was not only filled with a thick black haze, but I would say conservatively 10,000 flies were firmly entrenched in her living room.

Before we could do anything, I heard the front door open, and footsteps on the stairs coming closer. The only way I could describe the scream was, if someone was being skinned alive, while at the same time being forced to watch twenty five hours of Dobie Gillis reruns. It was blood curdling.

My father-in-law, at that moment, decided the best tactic was to go on a fly safari with a rolled up newspaper. By the way, she had white walls. I purposely use the word had, as did you know flies have blood just like mosquitoes? Rich, bright, red, blood.

At this point, I thought it best that we bid farewell and make a hasty retreat. My only parting recommendation was that if she repainted, she could tell everyone it was stucco.

We were walking up the block heading for my car, thinking we had made a clean escape, when the first of the fire engines sped by, followed by a second, then a third.

It seems that a neighbor, thinking the smoke was coming out of the apartment, instead of going in, decided to be a good Samaritan and called the fire and police departments.

Karen looked helplessly at me and asked, "What should we do?"

"Keep walking Karen. We've helped enough for today."

There was only one other time in my life I tried doing something involving "nature". The results were predicable.

I am an indoors man, this is an incontrovertible fact. If there was a religion called Couch Potatoes I would be its pope. It is for this reason, that when I agreed to go white water rafting with Karen and some friends, they were astounded, to say the least.

The place was Jim Thorpe, Pennsylvania, site of some fairly strong currents. This was a first for us, but we were assured that these rapids were safe and supervision was prominent. I was confident that all would be well. I am always confident all would be well and it never is. Today would be no exception.

It was five in the morning and we were on our way. Since it was a warm day for October, I wore only jeans and a tee shirt and I talked everyone else into the same. It was during that short period of time people still respected my opinion.

By 7:00 A.M. we were getting into our wet suits. I was already nervous as to just why they call them 'wet suits.' We were going to be in rafts, and I saw no reason why they would get wet.

By 7:30 we had already walked a mile into the woods. Here they had us huddled together with water yet to be seen. We were sitting in large, green, four person rafts, receiving instructions on everything that could possibly happen to us and how to handle it. It was like listening to a stewardess on a plane about emergency exits, and flotation devices, "Don't worry, this is in the unlikely event……"

The guide drilled into us, "If you fall out, don't stand up. Don't try to swim."

"What's left?" I thought to myself. "Karen is Catholic and can probably walk to shore. What was I supposed to do? I'm Jewish, I guess I could try parting it."

"Just lie on your back and float downstream, headfirst," he explained.

"Great, just great." My nervousness was now turning into anxiety.

"These plastic containers tied to the rafts are for your food, so it won't get lost," he continued. What does he mean lost? It's a small raft, how can it get lost? My stomach tightened as the anxiety evolved into trepidation.

He proceeded addressing the group. "Here are some extra oars in case you lose yours," he said, handing me five extra oars. "You hold them for everyone. You people look like you know what you're doing." He was an incredible judge of ability. Not only was this the first time I had ever even held an oar, Karen had to tell me it was the flat end that went into the water. And there were those words again, wet and lost. I was now approaching dread, as a wave of nausea swept into my belly. I was almost ready to say "Good Bye."

It was now show time! We had been indoctrinated, frightened and equipped. They now had us pick up the rafts and wait in line. Each group then walked around a bend, out of sight of the others. As we neared the bend, there was a strange mixture of sounds. I heard shouting and a distant clamor that can best be described as a muffled waterfall.

I had assumed that we would enter the river at a still bank. We would row lazily, getting used to the raft, the river and each other's rhythm. As we turned the corner, I saw what was creating the din. It wasn't a calm river at this point, it was Deliverance. All I saw was foaming whitecaps on raging waves roaring downstream. "Are they crazy?" I screamed to Karen over the thundering reverberation. "Karen, I never told you. I can't swim."

They were putting us smack dab in the middle of a major rapids. As you pushed your raft in, and jumped on top, the guides were screaming, "Row, Row, Row." It was chaos.

We were next. I stopped to discuss this with my group. I wanted to take a vote on whether we should continue, but after about five seconds of deliberations, the raft and we were in the water paddling for our lives. I was now well into panic.

Jerry, my best friend, and I were in the front with Karen and Joyce, Jerry's wife, in the back. We were the men you see and strength was needed to control us. For the first two minutes we were all right, rowing intently against the violent current. Karen was trying to convince me we'd be fine, and I was starting to believe her until I looked into the water and saw a head float by. Luckily, it was still attached to someone. Within five minutes, three more men had been thrown out of their rafts and were passing by us on their backs. I immediately became crazed and lost interest in this adventure and concentrated on looking for escape routes. Since I stopped rowing, the raft starting veering to the left, and we hit a rock ledge off to the side. I went flying out into the roaring waters.

There I was, out of the raft, hanging on with one hand, screaming for help. The liquid around me churning as if it was boiling. I had no pride. I screeched and shrieked so loudly they must have heard me back at the locker rooms. What I didn't know was at the same time that I was flipped out, so was the container with all of our lunch, as was the extra oars we were given for safekeeping. I subsequently learned a debate was in progress on what priority I was to be given. Jerry voted for the lunch, Karen said the oars, while Joyce wanted to save me. She was the only one that remembered; I had the car keys.

I looked up and noticed that as the raft spun clockwise. It was still being propelled forward, and we were headed for a direct collision with a rock wall. Given the speed we were traveling, I would be crushed between the wall and the raft. They could have taken me home in the container the lunch was in and that Jerry was currently groping for.

As we neared the wall, I closed my eyes and braced for the impact. Suddenly, I felt a hand grab me by the throat and pull me upward. Could this be God? Then I reasoned further. Would God grab me by the throat? Would God grab me by the throat while screaming, "Damn you, you Wimp, get back here in the raft and stop playing?" I think not!

What it was, was Karen. She leaned over, and with one pull of superhuman strength, snatched me from the jaws of certain death. I was in awe. I was in love. I was in shock. I immediately went limp and retreated into a catatonic state. I was relegated to the back of the raft with Joyce. Karen moved up front with Jerry and took control. I was reduced to a quivering mass, head in Joyce's lap, whimpering, wishing I was home.

We had quite a bit of river to go with no other way out. Steep, 1000 foot walls of cliff lined the chasm on both sides. It was starting to cloud up and get colder. Every once in a while, localized thunder-storms would break out with hail and lightening. Everyone just looked at me and kept saying, "All we need are jeans and a sweatshirt." What I didn't need was guilt at this moment. Terror was taking up most of my time right now.

We were now entering another long stretch of rapids. I was starting to sob now and just closed my eyes and prayed. I was never very religious, but at times like this, you try anything. I prayed to every religion of modern man.

Somehow we made it through and were almost to the end of this stretch when the raft hit a whirlpool, spun around and Jerry went flying out. A big guy, I thought he could just stand up and get back in. We slowed and looked around, but no Jerry. We were at a standstill and leaned over the side to look. Still no Jerry.

Karen and Joyce started screaming and crying. "He's dead! He's gone! He's dead!" was all they could say. I had my own problems.

"Charley!" screamed Karen. "Get out there and find him."

"Are you crazy? He's probably dead by now anyways. What can I do except die, also. Do you think they'll take us out by helicopter?"

Just at that moment, like Godzilla rising from the Sea of Japan, Jerry stood straight up, water flying everywhere, bellowing for us to help him. "Get over here," I screamed. "We have to get going. It's almost lunch time." He walked over, got back in, and we continued on our way. By this time the raft was so full of water, it had sunk below the water line. Looking at us from shore, all you saw were three people rowing, one body in back, floating downstream with no visible raft.

Finally, we caught up with our group as they had stopped for lunch. We pulled to the side, got out, and lay down on the riverbank to eat. It felt so good to get out. I had fleeting thoughts of staying there. Suddenly, the guides started screaming, "Back in the raft. Get back in the rafts." It turns out that the water was so high rattlesnakes were all over the riverbank. My feet never touched ground. It felt so good to get back in the raft. Suddenly it dawned on me, we had to go on.

I was getting flack from my three associates for not carrying my load. I think if a vote was taken they would have left me for dead along the shore. My own wife led the mutiny. I needed some more rowers. I needed help.

During the next few hours, people were floating by, who had fallen out of other rafts. They were the answer to my problem. I needed some of these floaters in my raft. We were always just a little late in getting to them. Other rafts kept reaching them first. After all, there were only three rowers in my raft. I desperately wanted another body. One or two times, I almost came to blows with another raft fighting for a survivor.

Three more hours past of rowing, spinning, banging into rock walls and whimpering. I did the whimpering, and then it was over. We were in the last stretch of calm water and we could see the end in sight. We hit the bank and I was out in a flash.

As a final act of indignity, they made us carry the raft up the side of the cliff to a waiting truck. We were wet, cold, hungry, tired, and no one was speaking to me.

On the way back on a bus, we saw the guide who had shown such confidence in us by giving me the extra oars. "So how'd you like it? Great trip wasn't it?"

It took three people to pry my hands from around his throat

9

KIDS-I WAS SURPRISED THE GOVERNMENT LET US HAVE SOME

Despite everything we had been through, we still decided we still wanted children. To be truthful, it was Karen that resolved that the curse probably wasn't genetic and it would be safe to bring a new life into the world. After all, what could happen to us having a baby? Millions of people do it every year. But then again, they don't live in Charley's World.

I was suffering through a tough first pregnancy. All Karen actually had to do was sit around and swell up. I had the tough part; it was my job to worry.

I worried about everything: Will the baby be premature? Will we ever choose a name? Will the doctor get to the hospital on time? Yet worst, will we get to the hospital on time. I had this recurring nightmare of having to deliver the baby myself in the back seat of my 1968 bright green Ford Pinto.

We lived only seven minutes from the hospital, yet I was still worried. It was for that reason I drove everywhere. Public transportation was out of the question. I even drove into mid-town Manhattan to my office which was, by no stretch of the imagination, an easy trip during the workweek. But on that Sunday morning, since I had to go to work, I thought it would be a relatively quiet day. I was very wrong!

As usual, I parked across the street from my office in an indoor, attended lot. I had long made friends with all of the attendants and made them aware that I had a pregnant wife and may have to leave at a moment's notice. I made it well known that I had big bucks for the man who got me out in less than three min-

94

utes when the moment came. They were all on standby to get me out ASAP when needed.

I was at my desk for a full ten minutes when Karen called and in a dramatically calm voice announced, "It is time!" Just as I had expected. It wasn't at 3:00 in the morning, when I was lying next to Karen, wide awake, waiting for her to say those words; it was when I was thirty miles away.

I was like a rat caught in a maze, banging into walls trying to find my way out of the office. It was as if I was one of those toy cars that hits a wall, backs up, spins around and tries again. I was in a frenzy, falling over chairs, knocking over plants and denuding desk tops of all of their paraphernalia. I left a swath of destruction marking my erratic path out of the office, down the elevator and out of the building.

I raced across the street, and jumping up and down screamed to the attendant "It's time…it's time!" He leaped into action. After all, he had also been waiting months for this. He raced downstairs banging into cars and walls along the way also screaming "It's time. It's time!"

After what seemed to be an eternity, I heard the comforting screeching of tires and the squealing of brakes coming closer, up from the bowels of the parking caves. Jamming on the brakes, he jumped out, I jumped in, and I was on my way.

The trip home took only twenty minutes doing eighty five on the Long Island Expressway. I was about a block from my house when I realized it was very hot and decided to adjust the air conditioner to make it more comfortable when she got in.

"Wait a minute," I thought to myself, "I don't have air conditioning." I looked around and found myself in the unfamiliar luxury of red leather upholstery in a bright white 1974 Cadillac Convertible. I never realized he had brought up the wrong car. True they were similar, a green 1968 Pinto does bear a striking resemblance to a 1974 white Cadillac, but I still should have noticed.

At that point I didn't care what car I had, I just wanted to get home. Grinding to a stop, I double parked, raced in, and found Karen in front of the TV, feet up, eating breakfast. "I tried to call back," she said, matter-of-factly between bites, "the contractions stopped."

I slowly and carefully drove back to the city realizing at this point I could be driving a stolen car if the attendant had reported it. I didn't care. I was tired. I was disappointed. I was depressed. On that Sunday morning though, when I came driving up the block, there was one happy parking lot attendant waiting for me.

While waiting for the baby to decide to become a member of this great society, we attended every course the hospital had to offer. Lamaze, child care, even one on breast feeding. I was asked to repeat this course when I asked the instructor if my Karen's nipples had to be boiled as did the bottles. To this day, I still don't understand why not! But, nevertheless, seven weeks later the baby was born in the hospital, healthy, with no perceptible problems except an extraordinary set of lungs.

Then a whole new series of problems presented themselves.

Laundry was the immediate problem. Karen, still on maternity leave, acquiesced to do my laundry since I was due in Washington D.C. that morning for a meeting at the federal agency where I was then working. Giving her this responsibility was in no small measure a minor risk. She had the habit of washing everything together; dress shirts, clothes, towels, sometimes my shirts came out speckled, like a trout.

But since it was such an important meeting, I took the chance and asked Karen to take extra care with the shirt I was going to wear. I wanted to look perfect; pressed suit, shoes shined, bright white starched shirt, perfect. Even on the plane down, I passed on breakfast for fear I would spill something. I sat absolutely still, lest I wrinkle my perfect look.

A short cab ride and there I was at agency headquarters. An impressive building, directly next to the White House. You could feel the power in the air. You could smell government at work.

I was well prepared for this meeting. As I looked around the huge, marble, table in the mahogany board room, there they were; the agency chief, my boss and a Presidential appointment, the agency comptroller, two congressmen, one senator and me.

I was at the head of the table. Rolling along in my presentation, everything going exceptionally well, I raised my arm high to make a point. A fatal flaw, an Achilles heel, a big mistake.

As I raised my hand, all of a sudden I felt something suddenly pop into it. As a magician materializes a rabbit, I was standing there holding a bright, red baby sock with a big yellow bear emblazoned on it between my thumb and forefinger. It was just hanging there. As usual, Karen had washed my shirt with the baby's clothes and one of his socks had hidden out in my sleeve just waiting for the right moment to present itself.

After a few seconds of silence, they stood up and gave me a round of applause. "Where's your birds?" someone shouted.

I was mortified. All I could think of was what I would do to Karen's washing machine when I got home. I checked my sleeve for other surprises and then continued on.

After the presentation was completed, one of the congressmen came up to me and said, "I bet you have a new baby at home."

All I could say to him was, "I'm lucky he's not a teenager. It would have been a size twelve sneaker flying across the room."

As our son Scott grew, the problems remained; they just change in scope.

We were living in Princeton, New Jersey and Scott was 3. We had decided to brunch at a very quiet, very expensive, very sophisticated restaurant. We thought it would be good for our son to start learning the 'social graces.'

The maitre'd showed us to our table, a nice one right in the center of the restaurant. The room, called The Greenhouse, was virtually bathed in sunlight by the numerous skylights and was packed ceiling to floor, wall to wall, with plants and shrubs. As we walked, we passed a myriad of very intellectual looking faces, most bearded, all deep in discussions with their companions. As we approached of our table, the maitre'd looked at my son and for a fleeting moment I thought he was going to say something like, "He's too young," but he never did.

We ordered our meal and as we waited for our food, we studied the surroundings. It was all very hushed and sedate. You couldn't even hear the conversations going on at the next table, but I'm sure talk of theater, books, government and other high topics were abounding. We had the only child in the restaurant and we talked of Big Bird and magic.

Scott loved magic. Every Saturday morning we would watch Mark Wilson, a popular magician on TV during these years. When the food came, Scott decided to show me a trick he had seen. He took a pickle chip from my plate, put it on the table, covered it with a napkin and, whipping the napkin off, expected it to be gone. Of course, to his dismay, it was still there.

He tried it two or three more times with no success. Finally, in frustration, he covered it, and yelled to me, pointing to the far end of the room, "Look at that." As I looked, he reached under the napkin, took the pickle and tossed it behind him. When I looked back, he pulled off the napkin, and lo and behold, it was gone. I was thoroughly amazed.

Amazed, until one of those bearded intellectuals from three tables down, came over, smiled and put Scott's magical pickle chip into my Bloody Mary saying "I believe this is yours."

Now I was upset. I scooped out the ping-pong pickle and was about to return it back to the gentleman's drink, when the maitre 'd appeared and suggested we finish up and, as W.C Fields said, "Vacate the premises."

We quietly left, feeling that Scott had absorbed enough social grace for the day.

Webster's dictionary defines the word panic as "a sudden overwhelming fright." Another incident involving Scott raised me to the highest levels of this emotion, both as for fear what had happened to Scott and to fear what Karen would do to me.

One Saturday night we were having guests, so as usual, Chinese food was on the menu. I took Scott with me to a local Chinese restaurant to pick up the food.

I placed my order and settled down in their waiting area, watching T.V, and munching on fried noodles. Scott loved fried noodles. He was wearing only a diaper, as it was the middle of summer and it was hot. He was just wandering around when after about 20 minutes they called my order. I claimed it and left.

When I arrived home and was bringing everything in, I had the strangest feeling they had forgotten something. I checked the order as I unpacked; Soup, rice, entrees, mustard, no, nothing seemed missing.

At that point Karen came in and casually asked, "Where's Scott?"

My blood ran icy cold. I started to sweat. I had forgotten him at the restaurant. I remembered the Egg Foo Young, I forgot my son. Without saying a word, I raced out to the car. Breaking every speed and driving law in the State of New Jersey, I arrived at the restaurant some two minutes later.

I ran in like a madman. I was breathing hard and had a glazed look in my eyes. I went straight to the waiting area expecting him to still be sitting there, but he wasn't. There was no Scott. All I could think of was going home empty handed and having to face HER.

What do you say? "Hun, we can always have more. Sweetheart, he's probably living with a nice Chinese family. Babe, don't worry, if he's still in there somewhere, he'll never go hungry."

I started to trot back out to the street after a quick scan of the restaurant, when out of the corner of my eye I saw a family of five sitting and having dinner. Nothing unusual, father, mother, a boy about fourteen, a girl seven, and a little guy, maybe two, in a diaper, sitting dipping fried noodles into duck sauce while jabbering away. That kid looked vaguely familiar. Getting closer, the little boy looked up, waved at me and went back to talking to the family. It was Scott, who within five minutes of my abandoning him had adopted a new family.

The mother smiled and told me they knew eventually I would come back. They were hoping it was before they ordered their entrees, as Scott wanted lobster.

Scott grew quickly and he reached the age that no matter how much I hated it we had to do all of those father/son things. We hiked, we canoed, we played soccer, we went fishing and believe it or not, we went camping. Needless to say, it was not an uneventful trip.

It is inconceivable to me why people like camping. Mankind has struggled for thousands of years to take himself away from caves and forests, to apartments, houses and Holiday Inns. Why is it that now, it is a such a macho thing to revert back? To go and purposely put oneself through the torment and inconvenience of camping out.

Yet every March, my son Scott's cub scout troop went North, to a scout campground where we were to have fun, even if it killed us. You must understand that my idea of roughing it is if the hotel doesn't have a pool. So, I put on my long underwear, packed up my asthma pills, toilet paper, newspapers, and television remote control *just for memories,* and at 4:00 A.M. that Saturday morning we were at the appointed gathering place.

I looked over some of the other fathers standing there; in Army camouflage, boots, Swiss army knifes hanging from their belts, drinking water from canteens, smacking each other on the back, talking over the good old days in the trenches. I stood there in my Lee's jeans, Polo turtleneck, Adidas sneakers, holding a trivial pursuit game, looking for someone normal I could make friends with now for later refuge.

"Let's caravan," the troop leader finally yelled. As each car fell into line, we pulled out. I was on the road ten minutes and already I missed my television and my couch. I fondled my remote control for solace.

Two and a half hours later we arrived. I immediately took inventory of the amenities. I expected certain things would be lacking, such as a swimming pool, tennis courts, and cable television. But some of the things I did expect, such as roads, walls and bathrooms were not there either.

After a treacherous ride over unpaved swamp trails, we arrived at the converted lean-to we were to call home for the next three days. Three walls and a roof, that's all there was, three walls and a roof. The bathroom was in a little house in the back. I think it's intolerable that we don't have a padded seat on ours at home, this one didn't even have a seat.

After we unpacked, we were all given various assignments. Cooking, cleaning, getting water; one by one, names were called and chores were assigned. I hugged the walls hoping they would miss me.

"Barron's, you do the campfire. Can you guys handle that?"

"Sure, sure, no problem," I blurted out. "How much trouble can throwing some wood into a pile and throwing a match onto it be?" I thought.

Everyone scattered to perform their various duties before lunch. After lunch the scoutmaster promised us a hike around a fifteen mile frozen lake. YUM! What a treat to look forward to. I'll have to figure out how to get out of that later. Right now, it's fire time.

I looked all over for the wood pile, but I couldn't find it. The scoutmaster was still with us in the lean-to. "Ken, where's the wood for the fire?" I asked.

"Right there, Charley," he yelled as he was walking out. He pointed to a bunch of dead trees at the end of the road.

I stood there with my mouth open. I had to go out, hunt and kill my wood. "This is barbaric," I thought to myself. "In New York, I picked up the phone and that evening a woodpile was waiting in my backyard." Out of force of habit, I looked around the room for a pay phone.

We found an ax, went out to that clump of trees, and begun hacking away. We managed to gather a bundle of dry limbs, brush and bushes. Slowly, I dragged them back to a strategic spot and made a pile. No one except Scott and I were around, so I used my best judgment.

I think the basic problem was, that I made the woodpile a wee bit too high and wide. By the time we finished, it was about eight feet high by six feet wide. It was amazing how quickly it ignited when I threw that match into it.

Everyone was surprised when they came back. It actually wasn't my fault. I had placed the wood in the center of the three walls in the lean-to. Who knew the floors were sawdust and not dirt? Who knew it would catch fire so quickly and spread to the walls? Who knew their car keys would melt?

Well, back to Scott and my 'fatherly attempts.' Strange as it was, they did not throw us out of the scouts for this event. They actually threw us out for something else. I had done the unspeakable; I had cheated at a scout competition.

When you have a ten year old son, the odds are you will be attending Cub Scout events. Every ten year old kid belongs to the Cub Scouts, it's required. I believe it's a federal law. I was in the Cub Scouts when I was ten. Unfortunately, I was discovered in a crap game at a pack night and I was drummed out of the corps. It was almost like a court marshal; they ripped off my bear patch and buttons.

I, of course, did not want this to happen to my son. So I attended every meeting, went on every outing, and entered every competition. The competitions were the worst. They were every father's nightmare. Your kid, wide eyed and eager, expecting to win, but of course something always went wrong.

After a while it got frustrating. You want to win for him so badly you can almost taste it. You would do just about anything to win, just once. But this was the Cub Scouts, an honorable institution. Cheating was intolerable!

After years of losing, we were now down to the wire. It was the last of the ninth with two outs. This, the last event, at the last pack meeting, in his last year in cub scouting. It was my last chance to win one for my son. It was the Pinewood Airplane Race and we were going to win, no matter what.

The premise of the race was simple. You construct a pinewood airplane out of a pre-cut kit. You are provided two thin rubber bands as engines, which must be wound very precisely the official number of turns permitted. The planes are then hung through a loop on a wire stretching across the length of the gymnasium, and then let go, racing against each other in heats, eliminating losers to the final winner.

I was determined. I was obsessed. I was going to win. The day of the big race was getting closer. The plane was in final stages of completion and it was turning out fairly well, but this wasn't a beauty contest. We were out for speed. I went out and bought three large, Mylar rubber bands, which I hid, deep in the body of the plane. I was going to win.

I finished the plane knowing full well it was in violation of the sacred rules of the pack. I should have felt shame, I should have felt embarrassment. All I felt was that I had to win.

The evening arrived and all was ready. The only final preparation was the winding of the engines. Forty turns you were allowed. The regulations were specific, forty turns and not one more spin. You were on your honor to comply. No one checked, no one watched, no one cheated. I smiled and started spinning my propeller.

At 300 turns, the three rubber bands were getting tight. At 350, I couldn't turn any more. I was going to win.

The plane was put on the wire next to our competition of three other planes. Three other puny planes with two, small rubber bands turned forty times. My son looked up at me. I was confident, I was proud. We were going to win.

The whistle blew, the propellers released, and the planes started revving. The other three planes buzzed, hesitated for a second or two, and then took off, moving smoothly across the wire. Ours roared so hard the plane vibrated, started moving forward an inch or two, then all of a sudden a flash, the plane streaked across the wire finishing a good five yards in front of the others.

We won. We had finally won. My son was beaming. He was happy. I was happy. All God's 'chillens' were happy. This elation lasted a full thirty seconds until I looked at the start line and saw our plane sitting quietly parked there. It never moved. How could this be?

Further inspection revealed that our engine was so powerful, it ripped right out of the front of the plane and finished a winner. Unfortunately, there is an archaic rule which states all engines must have a plane attached to them when crossing the finish line.

Tomorrow the sun will rise. Tomorrow the night will come. Possibly tomorrow, or the next day, or the next, my son Scott will come out from under his bed.

And come out his bed he did, and got me involved in another one of my favorite things, baseball.

Scott joined little league. He was twelve and wanted to play baseball. This was fine with me. I knew it had inherent responsibilities. I knew I would have to go to every game and cheer. I knew I would have to take him and pick him up from every practice. I knew all of this.

One evening I received a phone call from his coach. "Mr. Barron, Scott's first practice is tomorrow at 6:00," he said cheerfully.

"Fine," I answered. "I'll drop him off."

"Don't you mean you'll come with him? You're my Assistant Coach," he calmly corrected me; "I'll see you at 6:00." What I didn't know is that Scott had volunteered me as an Assistant Coach.

I hate baseball. I don't watch baseball. I don't even know the rules of baseball. All I knew was that sometimes you took your kid to a game, sat there and prayed it would rain so you could go home and plop yourself in front of the television to watch a real sport; professional wrestling. All of this was happening while you munched on a three dollar and fifty cent semi-raw hot dog, and a five dollar watered-down super-sized Coke.

Now, I'm Assistant Coach. I had a jersey and a cap. My number was 00, which I felt was very appropriate. The team called me Coach. Great!

At the first practice, the real Coach, John, asked me to take a couple of the kids over to a side field and practice pop-ups. After one of the kids explained to me what pop-ups were, I started throwing high flies to them, to practice, I assumed, catching them.

One of the kids, a myopic, red headed, ten years old, with glasses so thick I didn't know how he kept his head up, shouted, "Throw one to me, Coach."

"O.K. here it comes."

I threw a high one about twenty five feet over his head. He looked up, watching it come down. He was in perfect position, he was right under it, and he was looking straight up. Unfortunately, his hands were at his sides, and it hit him smack in the face. I spent the rest of the afternoon in the emergency room with him. My first coaching note to myself, teach them to put their hands in front of their faces when catching fly balls.

I showed up at the next practice prepared. I had a five-pound bag of ice with me. The Coach was late, but the team wasn't. There I stood with twenty kids waiting to practice and me. I had two choices; teach them accounting or start them on some sort of baseball stuff. I had them do the only thing I knew, run laps. I became an expert on laps in high school.

After 120 laps, they looked like they wanted to do something else. I was about to tell them a Babe Ruth story, when I saw Coach John's car pull up. Thank God, I was about to be relieved. John walked slowly up to me and the first thing I noticed was that he didn't have his Jersey on. He had it in his hand. The big O, the coach's shirt, was in his hand. My blood ran cold.

"I'm sorry Charley, I have to go out of town for about 3 weeks. You'll have to take over for a while." Those words still echo in my head. He just turned around and left. I was back to staring at those twenty faces.

There was about thirty minutes left of this practice, nine more practices, and three games, in that three-week period. That's an awful lot of laps.

I had a brainstorm. In my car, I had an easel with a large flip chart. I had used it earlier in the day at a presentation. I brought in on the field, had everyone group around and started drawing schematics of strategy.

"Does he know this is baseball?" some wise guy yelled out.

Scott, head down, walked over to me, took me behind the easel, and quietly told me, "No charts in baseball, Dad, just football."

"OK. That's enough for today. Just wait over by the curb for your parents. Be here early next time. We have a lot of work to do." I packed up and left. I was in trouble.

I had to think, I had to think. What would an intelligent, modern, American man do in a case like this? I had to do something I disliked, knew little about, and cared nothing about. The answer came to me in a flash; hire someone.

I remembered that last year when Scott was in soccer, the brother of one of the team members was an Assistant Coach and he was also a paid baseball umpire. It was worth a shot.

"Hello, is this Fred?"

"Yes."

"You probably don't remember me, but how would you like to be my Assistant Coach in Little League, for the next three weeks."

"I'm sorry, I really don't have......"

"I'll pay twenty bucks a week," I interrupted.

"Huh?"

"I will pay twenty five dollars per week, for the next three weeks to help me coach a baseball team. I'm desperate".

The practices went wonderfully. We won two of the three games, and when John came back, they were actually disappointed. They never knew for the last three weeks, they had a professional, paid coach.

Since we were having such success with Scott, we decided it was time for another. Our definition of success was simple; Scott was 4 and we were all alive and no one was in jail for child abuse. Actually I came close to the child abuse part. I was accused of abandonment. One evening Karen received a call from Child Welfare Services in New Jersey where we were then living. "Is there anything we can do? We can help you press charges and get child support," they offered. Karen astounded, asked them what they were talking about.

"Your son, Scott, admitted to his teacher yesterday that your husband left you. It's all right. It's nothing to be ashamed about." "He is in Dallas on a business trip. He'll be back tomorrow," Karen confided. They ended the call quickly.

Despite the fun of having one, we decided we wanted two. I believe the medical term is masochism. When we found out Karen was pregnant again, the doctors thought because of our ages, it would be prudent for Karen to go for amniocentesis. For those who never heard this term, it is a process whereby they take a three-foot needle and jam it into the swollen belly of a pregnant woman to suck out some of the fluid the baby is floating around in. Supposedly, they can tell you all sorts of interesting things about your baby including its sex and if it has certain types of diseases.

This sounded like a fun thing to do on a rainy afternoon, so we decided to go. Actually I decided and Karen agreed when the three guys took her bound and gagged into the outpatient surgery room.

As Karen was being prepared for the procedure, by now we had taken off the handcuffs, Margaret, the nurse working on her. She asked another nurse in the room, "whose doing the procedure on Karen here, this morning?"

"Dr. Habib," was the reply.

Margaret looking incredulous just said, "Oh my God!" and left the room.

Karen turned so white you could barely see her on the sheet, started mumbling something, got up off the table and started getting dressed. I knew we should have left those handcuffs on.

Margaret did return and saw Karen, who by now was headed for the door partially dressed.

"What's wrong Mrs. Barron?"

"What's wrong? The butcher of Westchester is going to operate on me. I heard what you said when the nurse told you it was Dr. Habib. I think I would rather have Dr. Kevorkian."

Margaret started laughing. It turned out that Dr. Habib was the head of the Genetics Department and does not usually do the procedure himself. And whatever doctor is assigned to the first case in a particular room usually stays there all day. Dr. Habib's own wife was the next patient in this room. It is very unusual for a doctor to treat his own wife. I guess Dr. Habib didn't trust any of the other doctors either.

The procedure went fine, the baby was fine, and of course, I had a Barron episode at the actual delivery. By the time Tara was born, Lamaze was in vogue and Karen wanted me to share the delivery. I had heard horror stories from friends of fathers passing out or just generally acting wimpy and making complete fools of themselves.
But considering the fact that this doctor already thought I was a maniac from my visits to his office with Karen, I had nothing to lose.

After spending six hours in the labor room comforting Karen, showing her how to breathe per our Lamaze classes, and generally trying to be compassionate, we were ready to move on to the delivery room. I believe the nurses used as a gauge that Karen went from verbally abusing me with some four-letter words I had never even heard put together in a sentence, to her attempt to get off the table and hit me with the bed-stand in retribution for getting her into this condition. I believe the medically accepted threshold for movement into the labor room is that she can curse and hurtle the table at least twenty yards in a concurrent motion.

I was shuffled into the dressing room adjacent to the operating suites and put into a paper gown, paper hat, paper booties and a paper mask. If anyone were permitted to smoke near me I would have gone up like a roman candle. I then pushed open a door and went into the delivery room.

There was Karen, covered from head to waist in sterile toweling with only her abdomen showing. As soon as I neared the table, a nurse sauntered up and holding a pair of gloves, motioned for me to put them on. There were about four other people in the room, but the nurse guided me right along side of Karen next to her abdomen. I thought this was strange. Although I had never seen it up close and personal, I had always heard that the baby pops out from an area somewhat to the south of where I was.

All of a sudden the nurse next to me handed me a scalpel. "Whoa!," I thought to myself. "I knew this doctor was cheaper than the one we used for Scott, but I didn't think it was going to be do it yourself." Stepping back, I told the nurse in the most professional way I could that I thought there had been some mistake. "Not me, Not me. Not me!"

It goes without saying I had screwed up. I was in the wrong room. I was standing in front of a complete stranger in need of a cesarean which they wanted me to do. Obviously they had mistaken me for her doctor. I ran like hell!

I finally found the correct room and carefully checked the face of the person on the table. It was Karen. "Glad you could join us." quipped her doctor, "Stop off for lunch?" Taking my proper place near the foot of the table, I tried to position myself to see the action through a mirror above the table. Not getting a good view, I inched my way down to where the action was until I felt a tap on my shoulder. "It's me or you kid," said her doctor. I had unknowingly positioned myself directly in front of the doctor. I probably could have handled the delivery. After all, I just finished a cesarean.

I moved, the baby moved and within minutes all was over. We now had two.

By the time anyone reads this, I may be dead. I am embarking on one of the most hazardous assignments one can perform for God or country. It is one so laden with risk and danger that few men accept, and less fulfill intact of mind and body.
Am I going off to fight on some foreign soil? Am I becoming an undercover drug enforcement agent deep in Colombia? Am I volunteering to test some new, highly contagious, live vaccine? No! No! No! It's something far more hazardous, far more deadly,…I have begun to teach my fifteen-year-old daughter how to drive.

It all started one early Sunday morning. A bright, clear day that I thought would be ideal time to start our lessons. Drew, my seven year old, asked if he could ride along in the back seat. "Why not?" I told myself. Little did I know of the jeopardy to life and limb to which I would be exposing him. True, it is a standard shift car, and on such it may be somewhat harder to learn driving basics, but nothing was an excuse for the pure physical abuse inflicted on us during that first forty minute lesson.

It began innocently enough. Tara got behind the wheel, put the key in and turned the ignition to start for a full two minutes. It is incredible the nerve wrenching, eardrum crushing sound two minutes of an overheating starter engine can make. I tried pulling her hand away but it was frozen to the key. Putting my foot on the steering column for leverage, I managed to get her from turning the starter into a metallic version of shredded wheat. We were now off and running. Off and running, bucking and lunging, jerking and thrusting, trying to find first gear. I know it's there. I had one a few minutes before when I was driving. I probably will not have one if we go another block or two in this manner.

"Tara, stop! Please stop the car."

"I can't. I don't know how to!" she screamed.

"I'm bailing out. Make room." Drew was now trying to escape from the back seat via a route which took him directly onto my head and out the passenger side window. It has been three days now and I still have the sneaker tread marks across my forehead. I can't blame him though. The only experience close to what we were going through was being in the wash cycle of a 1963 Kelvinator washing machine. How I know this is another story!

She finally found first and we were cruising along at five miles per hour when I felt some turns were in order. "Make a right," I directed. She promptly turned left.

"Make a left," I conceded. She obediently turned right.

"Why don't you listen to me?" I screamed.

"You have to remember," she calmly explained to me. "Your right is my left, and your left is my right."

It was time for some alley driving!

I headed for the parking lot of a nearby shopping center. Plenty of room to get the feel of the car was my reasoning.

She was doing fairly well until I noticed she was heading for a parked car. There was 500 acres of deserted parking lot, yet she found the only car there and was headed directed towards it at thirty.

"Stop! Stop! Stop!" I just found myself screaming with no slowing down in sight. When we were within five feet of it, she jammed her foot down on the power brakes as hard as humanly possible. It is truly amazing the impact the human face can take without any major permanent structural changes. After climbing down off the dashboard and wiping the minor blood traces off the windshield, I felt it was enough for one day and we headed home. I didn't want to wear her out.

I'm sure my nose will someday return to its original size and the nausea will go away. I'm sure once the starter and clutch are replaced the car will run as good as new. I'm sure Drew will at some point get into a car again. But look to the roads! Protect yourself! For, I'm also sure someday, Tara will have her driver's license.

Today my daughter Tara took her driving test. For the past 12 months, ever since getting her learner's permit, I have had the unique opportunity of giving Tara driving lessons. In truth, actual driving was about fifty percent of the total time I spent together with Tara. Repair and replacement took up the rest of our time. Filling in trenches on lawns and re-seeding, replacing mailboxes, landscape tie walls, several small pets, and in one instance, providing psychological outpatient care to an older woman who will never again be able to cross the street holding bags of groceries, accounted for much of our efforts.

Despite the public outcries, newspaper editorials, petitions, and the torch-bearing village folk demonstrating on our lawn, the day Tara hit 16 years of age, we went for the big test. In Tennessee driving tests are given at the Department of Public Safety, which seems incongruous. If it was really dedicated to the health, welfare and safety of the general public, they would be banning Tara from driving not about to condone it.

So there we were; the first ones on line at the testing site. I'm not sure who was more nervous, Tara or me. She worrying about passing or failing, I was wondering if you caused the demise of a state trooper during a driving test, would it be a felony.

The doors finally opened and there we were, standing at the counter signing in for the test. She was so innocent, so vulnerable, so trusting. She was so unaware of the fate soon to befall her. Tara was tense, too, but I really felt sorry for that trooper. Trooper Molly McQuire was her name. A nice name, a pretty lady, young…so young!

After filing out several forms, she was ready. "Tara, let's go," the trooper cheerfully called out. She was so happy, I felt so guilty. It was close to Christmas and I wondered if she had children. I guess the state would provide for the next of kin…. but was it a felony?

She must have done this a thousand times before, but couldn't she sense that this time would be different? My God, where was that survival instinct? That element of self-preservation that separated us from the chimpanzees.

First, she went through a safety checklist to see if the car was operating properly. Didn't she realize it wouldn't help her? Perhaps if she had a portable air bag…?

"Tara, turn on the headlights." Tara turned on the windshield wipers. "Tara, step on the brakes." Tara signaled left. "OK, Tara. Let's try a little driving." She started to sound a little apprehensive! Trooper McQuire was starting to catch on.

I was inside looking out through a large picture window with a woman and her daughter who was waiting to take the test next. "I hope someone else is available to carry on," I thought to myself.

"Back up!" Trooper McGuire ordered. Since the car was facing towards the building and to the right was a dead end, I really expected to see the back of the car swing to the right so she could leave the lot. The rear end suddenly swerved left and Tara was facing a dead end with nowhere to go. Wanting to give her another chance, Trooper Molly asked her to pull back in and try again. She did, with the same result. As was the next three tries. Eventually, we saw the doors open and Tara and the trooper exited the car and started for the building.

"They don't give much of a test down here," the woman standing next to me remarked to her anxious daughter. Obviously, new to the state, she thought in Tennessee you just pull in and out of a parking space a few times and that's it! Obviously she planned on spending most of time in malls and not the highways of this fair state.

That night trying to console Tara after learning she failed the test, my wife reasoned, "Now you know what to expect next time. You know the route and you can better prepare."

"What route?" Tara screamed. "I never made it out of the parking space."

At least it wasn't a felony!

Of the three kids, Drew, very early on, showed evidence of either developing into a shrewd businessman or a major player in the Mafia. Charging his siblings to "keep quiet" about various indiscretions (extortion), loaning them money at exorbitant rates (loan sharking), and searching the house including drawers and pockets to accumulate massive wealth in loose change (petty theft), qualified to become a member of just about any crime family in the country. He even dabbled in arbitrage.

When Drew was seven, he lost a tooth. This is an insignificant occurrence to the rest of the world, but to him it was a milestone. Yet even more important than the metamorphosis from childhood to adolescence, this event trumpets the financial thought processes at work even at this tender age.

"How much will I get?" was his first question when told of the tooth fairy. Whether he accepted her existence was never an issue. The cold, hard value of his tooth was his concern.

Quoting current rates I obtained from some friends already dealing on this market. "Two dollars," was my answer. He seemed agreeable, but decided to check this with his seventeen-year-old brother and fourteen-year-old sister. The answers he received were fifty cents and a dollar, respectively. You could see inflation at work here affecting even the open tooth market.

I had checked each of three nights but I still had not found a tooth placed under his pillow with the childhood anticipation I had expected.

"Drew, don't you want the tooth fairy to take your tooth? Don't you want your money?"

"Sit down," he said somberly. "I have a better idea." I sat wondering what his revelation was now. "Why not collect all my teeth as they come out and keep them in the box at the bank. If they are two dollars now and were fifty cents for Scott, what will they be worth when I'm ten? I'll sell them then."

I was astounded. My seven-year-old was hedging with human teeth. His teeth. When I was his age, I would have removed every tooth from my head for a dime each, if I thought I could get away with it.

Is this really so unusual? Today's children are not really the children of yesterday. Twelve-year-olds having babies, nine-year-old drug lords, fourteen-year-olds divorcing their parents, fifteen-year-olds whose after-school businesses go public. These are "old people in kids' bodies."

What is so different about these times that force children to grow up in attitude, temperament and thought long before their bodies catch up?

Just close your eyes and think about the kaleidoscope of things passing in front of them day after day:

- Superman dies, but dinosaurs live.
- Moms go to work, but children run the house.
- Don't have sex, but schools give out condoms.
- You need trees to make houses, but you can't cut them down.
- Milk is good, but milk is bad.
- Go out in the sun, but sunlight can make you sick.
- Eggs are good, but eggs are bad.
- Dad can smoke, but smoking is bad. Dad can drink, but drinking is bad.
- Don't take drugs, but mom takes a pill to calm herself down.
- Thou shall not kill, but you can have an abortion.
- If you're bad you go to jail, but if there's no room you can't stay.

- It's not if you win or lose but how you play the game, but you better win.

- If you want that you'll just have to save up, but I'm not going to pay you for doing your jobs around the house.

- Don't do that it will make you blind. Don't do that it will make you short. Don't swim there. Don't drink that water. Don't play with him. Don't go near her. Don't talk to strangers. Don't, don't, don't.

It's just too confusing to stay a kid!.

Seven years later, returning home from the office, I found Karen sitting in the living room with a sardonic smile on her face and a Bic pen in her hand. "See this pen?" she asked. "I found out today I'm pregnant again, and if you don't make an appointment for a vasectomy, we'll do it now, with this." I called the doctor that evening.

A man visiting an urologist for the purpose of discussing his vasectomy is unlike any other visit to a physician he could ever have. First, you're not sick. You are there for the express purpose of discussing someone assaulting the most personal and sensitive part of the male anatomy with a sharp instrument, and for this you must make an appointment and pay an incredible amount of money. It's like a catered mugging. You are paying this guy to disconnect you from something you have been using extreme methods for years, to protect. It is unnatural!

The terror of my visit started long before I even saw the doctor. While I sat in the waiting room, the nurse cheerfully came over and handed me a brochure she said I must read before I would be able to go into the inner sanctum. Fine, I had no problem with this. It was probably information on insurance restrictions for the procedure. That's all they think about is money......And then I opened the brochure. It was a twenty page, step-by-step, color, illustrated manual on exactly what the 'Westchester Slasher' was going to do to me. I made it to page three where he was injecting the anesthesia into a place I hardly ever touch myself for fear of self inflicting pain. He was using a six-inch needle.

I was about to make a run for the door when the nurse body blocked me and told me it was my turn. "Look," I begged, "just give me a knife and a room. With this manual I can do it myself."

"Please come this way, Mr. Barron." Her grip on my arm was like steel. If she would have grabbed me where the doctor was planning on grabbing me, they would have turned into diamonds in seven or eight minutes. I think I saw Super-man do that once in a movie.

She left me alone in a small room to read my booklet, and I heard her lock the door behind her. I guess this was the vasectomy waiting room, the only one with a lock. A short time later there was a knock at the door. Don't ask me why he knocked. I was locked in and I was knocking to get out. It sounded like dueling bongos. Finally, he came in.

"And are we ready for this procedure?" he asked. "Does your wife agree with your decision?"

I proceeded to tell him how afraid I was of going to bed, as she just laid there all night looking at me, patting her now swelling belly and stroking her Bic.

I think he understood just how in agreement she was with MY decision. "O.K. we're on." he said, rubbing his hands together. "Drop your pants."

"Are you going to do it now, here?" my voice raising an octave and starting to quiver.

"No, no, no. I just want to check the boys out. Make sure they're all right."

He looked like a Jewish tailor checking the material on someone's jacket. Star-ing at the ceiling, he inspected every inch of surface area between his thumb and forefinger while saying, "Nice, very nice." I've never even been that intimate with myself, let alone let someone else. Well, maybe just that one time when I was locked in the basement for a day and a half....That's another story! After coming up with a topographical map that put NASA's Lunar maps to shame, he told me to meet him in the hospital's outpatient wing, one week thereafter and shave myself clean. He did not mean my face.

The night before I knew what had to be done. I would just as soon let Karen near this site with a razor, as I would Lorena Bobbit. I lathered, shaved, and made a fatal mistake that involved some after-shave lotion. And off I went.

Lest us not get into details of the actual procedure, but I am sure Dr. Mengele, a close associate of Adolph Hitler, had something to do with its development. If I had known any secret information I would have been singing my heart out in a soprano voice.

Three months later I was to bring in a sample for analysis to make sure the operation was successful. This is how the telephone conversation with a female technician at the hospital lab went:

Me: I would like to bring in a semen sample for analysis after a vasectomy.
Them: That's fine. It must be no older than twenty minutes.
Me: I live a half hour from the hospital.
Them: "It must be no older than twenty minutes.
Me: I could have an accident driving with one hand.
Them: It must be no older than twenty minutes.
Me: Do you think you could help me out during your coffee break!
Them: CLICK

10

MOVIN' WITH FRIENDS

With two kids the apartment was no longer big enough, so we needed a house. It was our first house. We had bought a condominium in New Jersey. We were packing up and moving from our small apartment in New York City. We had two kids, a dog, a house full of furniture and other assorted belongings. All we needed now was a mover.

I called several of the major moving companies, one of whose estimator appeared at our door the next evening. A big, beefy Irishman named John Clancy came wheezing into our apartment after climbing four flights of stairs.

He immediately informed us, "There's a surcharge ya know, you're so high up".

"A good beginning," I thought. He continued walking around, room to room, casually making notes while sucking his teeth and clicking his tongue.

"Ya got some heavy stuff," he mumbled.

"Damn," I whispered to Karen. "I knew we should have gone with the cardboard bedroom set. It would have been so much cheaper to move".

After about 15 minutes, he grunted, "I'll be in touch," and left.

About an hour later, a small, fragile-looking older woman walked in. She too was from one of the larger movers. Gray hair, pale complexion, china blue eyes, big warm smile, Granny was giving us an estimate. I liked her immediately. She would be fairer. She would be understanding. She would be cheaper. Her name was Agnes.

Agnes first had tea, chit-chatted, then walked room to room commenting how lovely the apartment was, how tastefully furnished, and what an easy move this will be. She never wrote, never clicked her tongue and never sucked her teeth.

She left saying she would be in touch, leaned forward and whispered "I like you kids. I'm going to give you a good price," winked and left. I liked Agnes. I trusted Agnes.

We waited for the estimates. My brother-in-law Billy insisted we could move ourselves easier and cheaper. Since I had never done it before, I wanted professionals. Besides, Agnes liked us.

About one week later, John Clancy's estimate came. I opened it cautiously, knowing it would probably be high. He said we had heavy furniture. My guess was $500.00. After all, we had two and a half rooms of furniture with twenty boxes going from Queens, New York to New Jersey.

"No," I thought as I opened the envelope, "probably $200, after all there are federal laws governing movers." It was $2000.00! I couldn't believe it. Where's Agnes? I need Agnes.

The next day Agnes' estimate arrived. I held the envelope, it felt right, and it felt cheap. I opened it knowing confidently, Agnes liked us. As I opened, unfolded and read it, my anticipation became disappointment, my hope became despair, mighty Agnes had struck out. $2500 was her bid, I needed to call Billy.

We needed labor and we needed transportation. I rented a large truck from U-Haul, but help was another problem, I had to call in every chip I had. I begged my father-in-law, brothers-in-law, I beseeched my friends, and I cajoled associates at my office. All in all, I was able to gather together seven unwary helpers plus assorted wives and girlfriends, who were along, I'm sure, for snickering and amusement.

It was the big day, and at 8:00 A.M sharp. The crew arrived and we were ready. The first order of business, breakfast. We had to have the energy to continue. Finally, at about 9:00 A.M., we loaded the first of the boxes. Some of us brought boxes out of the building, some I stationed on the truck as loaders. We were very professional. I had the truck parked directly in front of the main entrance of my building. To achieve this I had to put my own car plus a card table and four chairs in the spaces to hold it until I picked up the truck that morning. I had to sit at the table all night, and even then, had three or four disputes with neighbors for these valued spots. After all, this was New York. The hard part was having my wife take over at the table until I got the truck.

The boxes took till noon. After all there were 210 of them. We had a lot of stuff. Then the furniture; we did have some heavy things, bedroom set, chairs, and my favorite sofa bed. I was on one end of the sofa bed, Billy was on the other. It was heavy and bulky. We had just come out of the apartment, made a sharp left into the hallway, down the stairs and headed for the building's front door. We were trying to turn the couch on its end to maneuver it out of a tight turn. All of a sudden I felt a sharp pain on my leg and a crash. I had forgotten to tie the bed down. There we stood, Billy looking at me, me looking at the sofa, now open and wedged tightly into the entrance doorframe. An angry mob of residents waiting to get out was now forming behind us in the lobby. Billy and I sat down on the bed to think over our plan; the neighbors started to shout obscenities.

Several of my entourage were now finished with their mid-afternoon break and wandered over. We formulated a plan to all get behind it and shove. It worked, although we took part of the front door frame with us. A small price to pay. The neighbors applauded and were happy to be released.

By 2:00 P.M., all was loaded. I slammed shut the door to the truck and our caravan headed for New Jersey. We stopped on the way for lunch.

We had been to our new townhouse only twice before, and although I remembered the inside, the outside was not as clear. I had sworn to all of my assistants that we could park the truck in the front and it was one or two steps into the house. We arrived at the base of a steep driveway leading to eighteen steps to the front door.

Everyone stood looking at the steps and then looked at me. I shrugged and offered them an additional late afternoon break.

By 6:30 P.M. most everything was unloaded. The group looked like the cast of <u>Night of the Living Dead</u> and was sprawled all over my living room floor groaning. I went out to the truck, climbed in and looked at the remaining item.

There it stood like some grotesque animal waiting to be walked. It was big, it was shiny, it was heavy, and it was a piano. My wife's baby; her pride and joy which she polished and protected long before she met me.

"It would live with us forever," she had said. Forever, if we could get it up these stairs.

Since everyone had collapsed inside, I thought I would help by moving the piano to the edge of the truck to make it easier to unload. With some effort, I was able to push it, just so two of the wheels were on the ramp, which led off the truck. I don't remember exactly what happened next, all I do remember is the piano groaning, and then taking off of its own accord down the ramp.

It started rolling, slowly at first, but began to pick up speed. I grabbed it as it rolled past, but it was just too heavy to stop. I hung on for about 100 feet letting it drag me, trying to act like a human anchor to slow it down. I eventually pulled myself up on top of it and rode it for another 200 feet before jumping to safety.

The truck was at the crest of a steep driveway which connected to another road just as steep which led to the main drag. The piano, as far as I could tell, was headed back to Queens. When my wife came out to check on me, she saw two things; one of which made her scream. To this day, I'm not really sure which she took to heart more. There I was lying at the base of the driveway, having collapsed from exhaustion after riding and chasing the fleeing furniture at least three blocks. I had come back for help. She also saw the piano, glistening in an orange sunset as it disappeared down the road and into the horizon.

Eventually, I did track it down. It had finally stopped about a half mile down heading onto a very busy four-lane highway. It had hit a light pole only a foot or so before entering onto this main drag. Luckily, it didn't make it into this road, as only a few yards up was the entrance to the Garden State Parkway and then who knows where it would have wound up.

It was fairly intact having suffered minor scratches and splintering around the leg areas. It did destroy a small wading pool in its path, whose only occupant, a small child, leaped to safety.

It took me three hours to push it back home with only Billy helping me. Everyone else ran like sprayed roaches when I told them the piano had bolted. The only reason Billy hung around was that I knew where he lived and in my maniacal state he was afraid I would track him down.

It was now midnight and very quiet in the condominium. My helpers having left, my wife sitting in the living room caressing her sick piano and quietly sobbing, while I was soaked in a hot bathtub thinking of all the wonderful things I could do to Billy for talking me out of doing business with my close friend, Agnes.

11

BUILDING A HOUSE-
ONLY HELL IS WORSE

One of the most traumatic experiences in one's life is buying, building, and closing on a new house. I have tried to describe in this primer, all of the essential elements, which create such terror, unknown to the average citizen, except in battle.

We were relocating to the South with my company, and the following saga is atypical of the New Home Syndrome.

Real Estate Salespeople

During their early boot camp training, one of the most important classes real estate sales people must conquer is Advanced Home Desires Conversions Techniques. This is basically the process of switching people from whatever they've visualized for the last twenty years as their 'dream house,' to whatever the office currently has in their listing book that is not moving. Two recent admissions to the Real Estate Hall of Fame honored one agent that convinced a family of five that it was more economically justified to buy the three bedroom the agent was showing them, and give away one of the kids to a relative, than to keep looking for the ideal four bedroom. And another who got the family to plunk grandma into a nice old age home than buy a two bedroom from another agent. These people are the giants in their field!

One January weekend, we ventured to Nashville, Tennessee on a house-hunting trip arranged by my company. We had decided on a moderate four-bedroom house, in a moderate neighborhood, at a moderate price. That's what we thought we wanted.

After receiving a phone call, we headed down to the lobby where a throng, or school, I never know what to call more than one, of real estate agents were waiting. We had taken this trip with several of my associates and all of us were being paired up with agents.

As we were coming down the huge lobby staircase and saw the waiting mob below, all I could think of were old jungle movies where large groups of piranha were waiting at river bottom for the poor unsuspecting herd of cattle to be driven down to them to be stripped down to their bones.

We finally found ours. It really wasn't difficult as she had a nametag on her chest that was so large I don't know how she was able to bend at the waist to drive. She was a cute, pert (I hate pert) blonde, named Missy. She had the same perpetual smile, etched onto her face that stewardesses had permanently implanted into them at training school.

She immediately stuffed us into her BMW (none of them ever drive Pintos) and told us we were the kind of people that needed to live in Brentwood, one of the most exclusive and expensive areas of the state. House after house she showed us, all very beautiful, all very large, all very expensive. She had good, good reasons why each of them would be THE house for us. But we stuck to our guns.

"Show me cheaper houses," I finally shrieked. "We're not Brentwood types, we're not good enough," I begged. "I don't eat croissants. I don't even like wine."

I heard an audible "Gasp" from the front seat. I thought she was going into cardiac arrest. Maybe I should have broken it to her gentler. Maybe I should have started with something like, "My hobby is raising chickens. I need lots of room" or "My son is in a rock group called Devil Men Flesh Eaters and they need small animals for sacrifices. Any farms nearby?"

She finally relented and took us to a less sophisticated side of town. She decided on a particular development she thought we would feel comfortable in. I expected the worst.

It turned out actually to be a nice house. At least the model was. As with all models, it had everything; special light fixtures, special trim, special paint, special plumbing, all extra. The key is, when you walk around looking at a model, to picture it naked. To picture it stripped of everything except the walls, this by the way, with some northern builders, is an option.

When we sat down to negotiate, I asked exactly what the options were. I was given a list, which was slightly larger than the phone book of Piscataway, New Jersey. "We make them almost custom built," was the answer. Great! So, what they were telling me was that the model will in no way represent what the finished house would look like. This can only be viewed in your own imagination. Maybe, we can get a police artist to draw it for us.

We decided to go forward anyway. We picked and discussed, selected and matched, envisioned and imagined, while they clucked and clacked about how wonderful our choices were. Even when we changed something they had previously said was perfect, they admitted our decision to change it, made it more perfect. It got to be fun after a while, never being wrong. I think I discovered how the Pope feels.

We finally finished and the price, with everything, was within what we had anticipated spending. I think we were going to make a deal. Once we had the contract dried off from the agents salivating all over it, we signed and the next phase kicked off. Getting the mortgage.

Bank Mortgage Vice-Presidents

The Mortgage Banker: Webster's Ninth New Collegiate Dictionary defines them as "a person whose sole job it is to loan you money, if you can prove to him that you have enough money and possessions to buy the house on your own if you really had to."

There is no person in a bank mortgage department who is below the rank of vice-president. This is a requirement of the job when they hire you. Secretaries, file clerks, or sales representatives, you must be willing to bear the title of vice-president. Not everyone can take the strain. Those who can work in bank mortgage departments.

The mortgage vice-president referred to us by the builder was Bob Billmoot. Bob arranged to meet us at our hotel room to fill out our application. Up to this point, the only professionals I knew that visited you in your room to service you were male and female escorts. I guess the net result of the services were the same anyhow.

He arrived and, sure as hell, had the same stewardess imprint on his face, a big, toothy, used car salesman smile. We chatted for a bit and then got down to business. "We had been pre-approved by the builder and the application was just a formality," he insisted. However, the questions included blood type, a family tree back seven generations, an EKG and I had to pee in a cup which he took with him.

I guess we passed, as by the time he left the room, he told us he would tell the builder to begin the foundation. We were approved. Of course, it was all subject to the results of the urine test.

Contractors and Sub-Contractors

We were approved by the bank, in our hotel room on June 15. We packed up the car, put all of our furniture and possessions into storage, and hit the road to live in a rental house, right near our lot until the house was ready. We arrived in Nashville on July 25th.

We immediately went to our lot. Since the builder had been given the go ahead almost six weeks before, we expected to see a framed house. The completion date of the house was October 15th. I have since found out that completion dates are not for real, only inside jokes between sales people and contractors.

As we drove up to the lot, I had Karen close her eyes so she could be surprised by how much was done. For all I knew, the walls and roof were on. As I got closer I was looking for the framed house, no house. I was looking for a completed foundation, no foundation. What there was, was a hole; a big deep hole with no other signs of life or activity. Karen, still with closed eyes, asked me if I was surprised. I told her to keep her eyes closed.

It took them six weeks to dig a hole. A perfect hole, yes, but not six weeks worth. Were they employing the handicapped? Perhaps the laborers were blind and dug by Braille. It must be something like that.

The next morning I was on the phone with the sales agents. "What's the story?" I asked. "There's nothing being done."

"Hunting season," was my answer. "It's a bad time to start a house. Monday we begin framing yours."

I believed that for now. I waited till Monday. I hoped everyone got their limit by then. Monday came…..and went.

MONDAY-The wood was there, no workers.
TUESDAY-The framers showed up, no wood. It was stolen.
WEDNESDAY-Half the men were there, new wood was delivered. We're getting closer.
THURSDAY-All the men, all the wood, finally together at last. Of course they took the day to discuss their successes during hunting season.
FRIDAY-We're really rolling now.

We had two solid days of work when the heat wave struck. Everyday, from noon to six or seven in the evening it was 105 degrees. When it's 105 degrees, the men don't work. I never understood that; these were Southerners and they should be used to this. I could see if these were men on loan from Fairbanks Construction, but they grew up in this weather. I would bet if it was 105 and they were running after a deer, they would have no problems. Anyhow, they worked half days for the next two weeks.

Work went slowly in August and September, speeding up somewhat in October. Sometimes the sub-contractors showed up, sometimes they didn't. Sometimes the materials showed up, sometimes they didn't. Sometimes mistakes were made, many times mistakes were made.

- A new opening to the crawl space was put into a garage closet via sledge-hammer versus cinder block. The plumber didn't bother to check under the deck where a nice, large, opening to the crawl space was waiting patiently. His response when shown the opening "Gol-lee".

- A small fire to burn debris set the deck on fire. "Unusually windy" was the explanation. Luckily two workmen were asleep under the deck at the time and extinguished the fire by pouring a case of beer on it.

- One morning, while I was standing watching some men putting up sheet rock, the insulation man came crashing through the ceiling above me. His answer, he tried to step on a cricket and there was no floor. It was fine though because he fell on the painters who were varnishing the railings.

The salespeople tried to charged me extra as the railings, now covered with insulation, were now treaded for safety and was on their options list.

- All of the carpeting on the second floor began to shed. I'm not talking of some odd piece of strand here and there. If this was a person, the Hair Club for Men would have considered this terminal.

Electricians, plumbers, linoleum men, roofers, carpenters, they all took their turns. From the ridiculous to the sublime. Mistakes, errors, miscalculations, and stupidity, I saw it all. I think these men learned their trade at the same school I attended, but for this I was paying, for so I found no humor in it. Despite all of this, the house finally was near completion. It was time to arrange for the closing.

The Closing

For two full weeks it rained. The front and rear yards resembled the Great Swamps of Florida and the ground was so wet it was actually bubbling. The problem was in order to close with the bank we used, all landscaping had to be completed. In order for the landscaping to be finished, it had to stop raining. My front yard was washing away, rocks and all, and they wanted landscaping.

The builder decided to try it anyway. I think that the fact that my commitment was expiring in two days and I was calling him every two hours, twenty hours a day, may have had something to do with it.

The landscapers showed up with sixty five assorted trees and shrubs. The appraiser was due in three hours to take a picture for the bank, of my beautifully landscaped house. We had to hurry. Off they went, three men, knee deep in mud, slipping and sliding, trying to make trees stand up straight in a rice paddy. It looked like mud wrestling, only they weren't pretty.

Just when it looked like they were going to make it, just twenty minutes before the appraiser arrived, just when each tree and shrub was standing semi-straight on its own accord, water came cascading down, sweeping away in its path, half of the greenery that was standing. The main water main had burst carrying my seeded lawn, straw, shrubs, one of the landscapers and other assorted things somewhere downstream.

The appraiser arrived shortly thereafter to see a barren piece of property, jokingly called my lawn. Fortunately, the builder knew the appraiser and he agreed to some trick photography. Enlisting the aide of my entire family, new neighbors, workman, and passersby-by, everyone grabbed a tree or shrub. They hid from view behind a house corner and at the count of three held their assigned plant life straight up while a picture was taken of some very nice standing shrubbery. When everyone let go, there it all went back downstream.

We did close and eventually a real lawn was installed, but it never looked quite as good as the picture.

12

CARPETBAGGERS HAVE ARRIVED

Being New York transplants in Nashville is conspicuous in much of our conduct, but none was so flagrant as my wife's shopping trip to a southern based supermarket, Kroger's, shortly after our arrival in this fair city.

While settling up at the register, she was casually watching the bagger packing up her large order and then turned her attention back to the cashier. When she finished, she looked for her groceries, expecting them to be waiting for her at the foot of the checkout counter. Alas, they were nowhere to be found.

She then noticed someone heading to the store entrance boldly making off with her order in an arrogant New York style larceny. Racing after him shouting, "Stop thief. Those are my groceries." She caught up to him in the parking lot and courageously confronted the perpetrator.

Just as she was about to pounce and wrestle away his booty, she noticed his blue Kroger's shirt and nametag, which proudly proclaimed that he was Bud, your friendly Kroger's Customer Service Representative.

After explaining Kroger's carryout service, she sheepishly led Bud to the car where he carefully packed up the loot into her trunk. To make amends, she produced a large tip handing it to him with an apology.

The young man smiling broadly proclaimed, "No need for that ma'am. Welcome to the South."

The transition between two such divergent cultures as Nashville and New York is indeed difficult at best. In New York one develops a survivalist attitude where you trust no one, you suspect everyone, and the overriding philosophy for survival is; "They want to take it away from you, you want to keep it. Do what you must." This is probably how it was in the Old West but without the glamour.

Instance after instance here provide glimpses of how it probably was when caution was unnecessary and neighbor trusted neighbor. Stores where checkout clerks, upon my instinctively showing a drivers license and two credit cards to pay by check, ask me curiously, "Isn't it good?" Self-service pastry cases where you fill up your bag and mark the price on the front with a magic marker. The restaurants where the house policy is that if you didn't enjoy your meal, you don't pay. Such attitudes, policies and perceptions, such lifestyle would soon become prey to the hustlers, con men and wise guys of the big apple. Such a gracious mode of living would soon evolve to the competitive, combative, survivalist fortresses all in New York endorse.

But here, for a while anyway, the checks don't seem to bounce as high, the right amounts are on the donut bags and most people still pay their restaurant tabs. Here, for now, it does work.

As the man said, "Welcome to the South…"

Three years ago I lived in New York City, otherwise known as the Big Apple. I paid New York taxes, I walked New York streets and I held a New York driver's license. For the uninitiated, holding a New York driver's license is tantamount to being classified as a '007-License to kill.'

New York drivers are infamous. Maneuvering a car through the borough of Manhattan takes a skill level that can be compared only to fighter pilots engaged in combative dogfights while simultaneously dodging enemy anti-aircraft shelling. Driving has become so much of a competitive sport there that, although on my driving test I cut off a bus, and went around it on the sidewalk as passers-by ran for cover, the examiner congratulated me for quick thinking and passed me with flying colors.

I was sure I had seen every type of road hogging, dodging, speeding and cursing known to modern man. I was sure I had been involved in every kind of near miss, close encounter and fender bender there were until I came to Nashville. A great place to live, nicest people I have ever met, until they get behind the wheel of a car, then watch out.

The first month I lived here I thought that half the cars on the road were each towing another car. Finally it dawned on me, they're tailgating. The rule of thumb is to stay at least one inch away from the car in front for every ten miles per hour you are going. And let us not forget that Tennessee state highway law dictates that on all Interstates one can only exit from the passing lane.

Within the first eighteen months here, Karen had three accidents and I had two. In each we were standing still. Karen's first mistake was being behind a fellow who decided to back up going about forty in order to go around the car in front. The second was in opening her door. Along came a Honda, who parked right beside her, taking her door off its hinge. My two were relatively boring by just being rear ended while standing at stoplights. Karen's third was unique even by New York standards. She was broad sided by a gentleman on a runaway rider mower careening down his driveway. My insurance company loved this one. We didn't know if we should file a claim under our State Farm collision policy or his Sear's extended warranty.

I also found out fairly quickly that the police do not like to fill out paperwork. No matter what the car looked like after each accident, it was an "under $250 damage report" that was completed. I had to laugh when Karen came home with what was left of the front door in the back of our Blazer and had an "under $250" report in her hand. I don't think I could get a cardboard door put on that car for $250. I would fantasize of a poor soul standing there with his new Jaguar, squashed to the size of a suitcase, and the cop saying, "Yep, a little buffing, some paint, $250 should be more than enough."

All in all, we have been 'southerners' for three years now and our closest friend is the owner of the collision shop. But come to think of it, he's not such a bad friend to have; he's the richest guy in town.

But I leave you with this warning. No matter how dangerous it is on the roads now: no matter how reckless drivers are: watch the skies, look to the horizon, a new champion is about to debut. She's tough, she's rough, and she's Tara, my 15-year-old daughter. She's currently in training but soon to be driving, beware!

Scott was growing, too. Probably faster than I would have liked. When you live in the South, you must love football. I don't!

It's Saturday morning. Here I sit with twenty-five other parents at my son's school listening to the head football coach. He is offering an impassioned plea to us, the parents of the 1994 varsity football team, on the importance of our attention to and participation in the football program. He told us basically that it is our responsibility to assure that our sons: attend all practices; attend all training; attend all games; eat right; sleep tight; keeps their grades up; their hormones down; and are pure in mind, body and disposition. After I accomplish all of this, I can fly off and save the world from Lex Luther.

I can't even get my Scott to clean his room, yet the coach wants me to guarantee he will be there every day to lift weights and go on forced marches around the campus. These are the ramblings of a head coach who has three small daughters at home instead of a hulking teenage son. These are the fantasies perpetuated by the overconfidence from having his every command obeyed. Such discipline is garnered by the looming cadre of assistant coaches under his command. Alas, at home it's only me. Poor little me!

Don't get me wrong. It's not that I lack parental authority. What I lack is the passion. The passion for football that the coaches, the players, the other parents and most of the population of Tennessee seem to have. I know it's a cardinal sin and downright un-American to have such radical thoughts here in the South. But for the life of me, I cannot get excited sitting and watching twenty two padded, greased and grunting guys, running up and down a field chasing elliptical pigskin and jumping on top of the unlucky soul who happens to be holding it.

In New York, where I was until three years ago, Major League Baseball is **the** sport. It is popular; it is talked about; it is the national pastime. But here, football is more than a pastime, it is an obsession. Orange flags flapping from every other car antenna, men walking proud with "Go Vols" tattooed to their foreheads, I'm sure some women have it, but in less obtrusive places. The Friday night high school scores were taking more evening news airtime than Bill and Hillary. Many a Monday morning I have tried to have an intellectual conversation over breakfast with a colleague on an exceptional Matlock episode, only to be overwhelmed by a critical analysis of a quarterback sneak in the Trotstown-Breckenridge junior high football jamboree on channel 88. I just don't get it!

I can't say I'm not trying. I go to all of my son's games (if weather permits), I watch as many games on television as I can (if they don't interfere with my favorite shows), and I read the sports page (if I can find it in the rubble of Scott's room.)

I have bought a little orange flag, not attached yet, and I am on a waiting list for a VOLS license plate. I even now know where Knoxville is. (Note: I will get the tattoo only if Scott gets a full scholarship to U of T.)

I want to get the passion. I want to get the lust. I want to like football!

13

HOME IMPROVEMENTS-
THE DEVIL'S WORK

I have done many things in my life that have imperiled my life, liberty and health. None without exception have approached the actions I have performed with blind, moronic enthusiasm and total ineptness in the name of home improvements.

With the best of intentions, and with the objective of doing it better and cheaper, I have executed events that have had as the most common result; allowed me to become very good friends with the men and woman manning the Emergency Room at the local community hospital. Moving out of our apartment into a house really sealed my fate. All of my life, I have been an apartment dweller. It's great! The toilet stuffs up, a window breaks, and you call the superintendent. He comes right over and fixes it. All of a sudden, I'm married and I own a condominium; not fully a house, but by no means an apartment. They only help you with problems you have outside. My pipes blow up, I'm on my own. I tell the landscape committee my trees have root-rot and 6 people show up. I don't understand. I need my superintendent.

We were living there about six months; Karen decides she wants the unfinished basement, finished. I had just bought my first screwdriver, for which I could not find an instruction manual, and she announces I am going to make some major renovations.

Off we were to the hardware store to buy our new basement. Between us we had half a brain as to what we needed and how to do it

With today's hardware superstores, as so as you walk in, one of their improvement consultants hooks on to you like a salesman at a new car showroom. He becomes your shadow. All I wanted to do was walk around and see if I could identify anything, but Tom insisted on helping.

First, we had to decide on the walls. I wanted to just paint the cinder block, but Karen had other ideas. She wanted paneling.

Tom asked, "Charley, I think he liked me, do you want below grade or above grade?"

"Above grade, of course," I told him. "I only want the best."

"No, Charley, is the room at ground level or below ground level?"

"My basement is downstairs. Is that bad?" I asked.

Tom just stared at me.

"Next", I continued. "I need the kind of nails to put the paneling onto cinder block walls."

"You need studs," he corrected.

"Nope, I'll be working alone," I answered. "No helpers."

Tom started staring again. I think he was starting to be sorry he selected us as we came in.

After Tom explained about all this wood I would need. He suggested I would need a couple of sawhorses to cut on. I told him I would take one; I know when I'm being conned. Karen can hold the other end of the paneling. She was nine months pregnant and her belly made a good level platform for holding it. Tom left us at that point, shaking his head and probably considering a new career.

We wound up buying wood, ceiling tile, nails, insulation, all kinds of stuff I hadn't really thought about. To help me get started, Karen's Uncle George came by. A great guy, smart, a corporate executive, but by no means as handy as me. He was invaluable that day though; he brought the handsaw.

We decided to begin with one corner of the basement which had to be boxed in, due to some air ducts petruding from the ceiling. It was the day of the baseball play-offs and we both wanted something we could say we finished, but in absolutely a minimal amount of time. We framed it out in no time, and then we started to put the paneling on. There we were working in tandem; banging away furiously. We were talking to each other, but I couldn't see him because he was on the opposite side of the wall.

Finally it was finished; a faultless corner. Unbelievable as it seemed, both sides met evenly in a perfect square. Better yet, we had plenty of time to wash up and see the game.

"George, it looks great."

"I can't really tell in here," George complained. "It's pretty dark. Open up and let me out."

"Open what up? It's a wall!" I screamed.

I suddenly realized that in our rush, I had sealed him into the corner; our absolutely perfect corner. He wanted out, but I had no intention of destroying the greatest piece of work I had ever done. I remembered there was a small opening where the ductwork went through the concrete. I tried to negotiate.

After about a half-hour of brainstorming, we tore it down. He was getting hungry, the game was almost on, and he threatened to kill me. It just seemed like the right thing to do.

I decided to start another day.

Living in an apartment was by far the easiest. A pipe breaks or the shower backs up, you call the maintenance man and he trots over and fixes it. Lawns and shrubbery are mysteriously taken care of when you are at work. As far as the garbage, all you need do is drop it into one of those neat little chutes in the hallway and it disappears forever. The condo was better since I didn't have to mess with the great outdoors. But when we bought the house, everything was my problem.

Moving into our first home was traumatic to say the least. You are expected to do everything yourself. I have never done everything myself! I was now forced to do all kinds of strange, mystical, and sick things. I had to plunge out toilets, sweep walks, and clean out gutters. I had to bring the garbage out to the curb, caulk holes and shovel snow. I had to do yard work, YARD WORK! Mowing, weeding, watering, and raking, I had to do it all. I hated raking leaves. I hated leaves. There were piles of these things everywhere. I almost had my wife Karen convinced that it was best just to leave them there, year after year as they eventually turn to topsoil which it is great for the lawn and expensive to buy. One conversation with her father killed that approach. She wanted me to get rid of them. What to do, what to do?

I contemplated my options. I could fill up my Pinto and scatter them throughout the neighborhood like some perverse Johnny Appleseed or just chuck them over the fence onto my neighbor's yard. Since my car was brand new and the guy next door was an ex-marine, I quickly discarded these alternatives. I could bag them up, gift wrap them and leave them in my car in New York City. They would surely be gone within a half hour. Too many leaves, too many trips, dissuaded me from that route, although I was sure it would work.

A friend suggested burning them. With my track record, did I really want to start a fire near the house on purpose? I decided I would do it, but I would use every precaution. I did everything by the book. I went to town hall and got a permit. I dug a trench around my new 50-gallon trashcan in the middle of the lawn, far away from the house. I had my garden hose on and ready.

I filled the can to the brim, lit a match and tossed it in. That's all it took. The leaves were so dry they ignited instantly. The fire spread quickly through the can and soon, intense orange and blue flames were shooting up sending yellow sparks skyward. I just sat and watched fascinated by the leaves being consumed. It was almost as if they were melting.

Suddenly, things were going wrong. Burning leaves were flying in all directions, flames shooting everywhere. A thick green ooze running aglow down the driveway flowed like hot lava.

It's all gone now. Cooled down and cleaned up. I did learn an important lesson that afternoon,…. never burn leaves in a plastic garbage can.

This was in New York. By the time we had moved to Tennessee, I had owned several houses and became quite the expert in many areas. That is, until we challenged the Southern version of Mother Nature-Mama Nature.

Today is Saturday and I have just finished putting twenty five pounds of grass seed on my lawn. Tomorrow is Sunday which means it will rain and wash the twenty five pounds of grass seed off my lawn. This is a ritual I have performed for the last five weeks. It has become tradition; it is my grass seed sacrifice to the rain gods; It is gardening in Tennessee.

I've had houses in other parts of the country where growing grass and maintaining bushes wasn't the feat of gargantuan proportions as it is now. I believe the critical factor was, that in these other locales we had an element which is missing here in the South. We had something which although basic to gardening is just not available in this part of the country. This mystical material is dirt. Plain, brown, worm-infested, mud pie making, gritty, nifty dirt. Here we have some sort of rock laden, dough like substance which in God's infinite wisdom he has passed off as soil to the good people of Tennessee. This, combined with the scorching heat of summer, torrential rains of the fall and spring, and that ever-present nemesis Bermuda Grass, we have a horticulturist's hell on earth, better known as the Gardens of Nashville.

Let us examine each of these issues separately;

DIRT—To the naked, uninformed eye it looks like dirt, it feels like dirt, it even tastes like dirt. Just looking at our lawn newly seeded by the builder, we were given the false sense of confidence that we will actually be able to plant and grow living things on this piece of property. In reality, the dirt is actually slate and rock surrounded by a thin layer of clay. This material is great for making bricks and adobe huts, but unusable for nurturing any form of life.

The truth is to grow anything you need mulch. Mulch is a miraculous compound composed primarily of shredded hardwood. To properly plant something, and to expect any life to be forthcoming, first you put the flora in peat moss soaked with root starter. Then you dump mounds of mulch over it. In effect the bush is suspended between the moss and mulch and should in no way come in contact with the dirt which in all probability would kill it.

WEATHER-Springtime in the South brings forth the golden leaves of the Bradford Pear, the crimson leaves of the Azalea and the flood warnings of the National Weather Service. Torrential rains cascading down the non-absorbing clay fields provide breathtaking views of flooded basements, overflowing river-banks and routine mud slides. After two or three months of this, Mother Nature dries us out during the summer months with 100+ degree-days with not a drop of moisture in sight. After three or for months of this, the skies open up provid-ing us with flood conditions again, but now on scorched, cracked earth devoid of any plant life whatsoever which, of course, provides us with even greater flooding.

BERMUDA GRASS-One tends to have mixed emotions towards this life form that has a philosophy akin to the Third Reich; it wants to take over the world.

Although during the cold of winter, Bermuda Grass has the color and consis-tency of newly mown straw; during the rest of the year it is thick and green and completely free of weeds. This is because it will not allow anything else to grow in it, near it or where it is planning to go.

All varieties of weeds, other species of grass, anything from the animal king-dom, and small children to undersized adults are in danger if they linger too long near the creeping tentacles of its vines. Across mulch beds, over concrete drive-ways, it is virtually unstoppable in reaching its destinations. Weed killers, grass killers, rat poison, everything short of a flame-thrower and Agent Orange is help-less against its intrepid migration. It seems to mutate from generation to genera-tion becoming immune to these toxic substances and in some instances even thriving on them. Bottom line, Bermuda Grass creates a beautiful lawn, but it is a living, thinking alien life force which you must respect and give it a wide berth for your safety and survival.

And so, this is the fun; the excitement and realities of gardening in this land of milk and honey. This is the challenge, this is the quest. Sometimes I think I'll just put down Astroturf and be done with it. But then again,……..the Bermuda Grass will probably eat it.

This was the summer fun of owning a house. I soon found out that the House Demons provide year round entertainment to the homeowner, and especially to me. I, of course, have my own guardian devil stalking me. In our mountain top home in New York during wintertime we kept our fireplace stoked up continuously. Wood was getting expensive, so I decided there must be a cheaper way.

While looking through a neighborhood weekly, I noticed an advertisement for a 'truckload of firewood' for $200. A truckload sounded like the answer to my problem, so I called.

"How much wood in a truckload?" I asked.

"Oh, about three cords. Keep in mind though; they're bigger than the twenty four inch length fireplace logs. You may have to cut them," the voice on the other end explained.

"That's no problem, I have a chain saw," I proudly told him. "No problem. at all."

"O.K. We're on. How's tomorrow at 3:00 P.M.?"

My wood was on its way. Karen kept asking me why it was so cheap. She always doubted my decisions. She always had this pessimistic gloom & doom attitude

"Don't worry," I reassured her. "I'll have to do a little cutting, that's all. He said they weren't quite fireplace width. That's why we bought the chain saw, for things just like this."

I went to the garage and oiled my chain saw. I was ready.

The next day was Sunday. Actually, I had forgotten all about the wood, and around 2:30 we were all sitting down to dinner with some friends. Suddenly, a barely perceptible tremor rattled the windows. Not enough to even see, more as if you were feeling it. Growing in intensity, the house started shaking and dishes were sliding off the kitchen table.

It kept getting louder and louder, to where you had to hold your ears and yell to be heard. We all ran outside to see if a 747 was landing in the front yard. The roar was reaching a crescendo, as the largest truck I had even seen in my life, pulled up the road, directly in front of my house. It was as wide as the entire road, and about twenty feet high.

A grizzly, bearded, man loomed down at us from high in the cab and shouted, "You Barron? I got wood for Barron. Where do you want it?" There was no way he could get into my driveway with this dump truck from hell, so I pointed him to a small parking area across the road. He maneuvered into it and began to dump.

As the rear end started going up, I knew we were in trouble. Raised, the thing was probably forty feet high. He got himself jammed under and into a telephone pole. Lowering the bed, he brought the entire top part of the pole down with him, which I found out later, cut telephone service to about 200 people including myself.

He now moved forward and tried again. Now dangerously near power lines, I closed my eyes and pictured us causing another major blackout up the northeast corridor. He cleared the pole but not the cable lines that had been put in only three days before. I knew there would be no HBO tonight for the same 200 people. I was going to be the most popular person on the mountain.

He began dumping. I was amazed at what came out of the back of that truck. Stumps five feet high and ten feet across came out with a roar. He was jettisoning a load of trees into the parking lot. There were at least twenty five of these redwoods lying in every direction. One had even rolled out into the road. My son Drew stood behind one, and you couldn't eve see him. These were big suckers.

After he left, I just stood there, almost eye to eye with this forest, wondering what the hell I was going to do. True to form, Karen came up behind me holding my ten-inch chain saw, handed it to me and sarcastically asked, "We'd like a fire tonight. Think we have enough wood?"

She was also worried that if we left the wood there overnight, someone would steal it. We all looked at her as if she was crazy. You would need a flatbed truck, and a crew of five to steal just one piece.

After working on one piece for six hours, I finally determined I had to get some help. I needed men with heavy-duty equipment to cut and move this stuff out of my neighbor's driveway. I'm positive he would notice a new National Park, next to his house.

The bottom line was:

Cost of wood	$200
Cutting & moving	$300
Telephone pole repair	$250
Cable repair	$100
Removal of wood in road	$50
Scrap cleanup (dumpster)	$100
New chain saw	$150
Total discount wood	<u>$1150</u>

Since three cords of wood, delivered and stacked would have cost me about $400, I knew I was going to hear about this one for a long, long time.

The house in Tennessee brought with it all kinds of revelations. I had to face things I had never even heard about before. I had to face new terrors such as the crawl space; a miraculous invention of builders to keep homeowners on their best behavior. When something goes wrong which requires your crawling into this surrealistic cave, if you are on good terms with the builder, he'll send someone to fix it. Otherwise, you must enter this cramped, mind-boggling, confusion of pipes, vents, conduits, wires, insects, and snakes yourself. Only Alice, in that fabled looking glass, knows this horror.

It was a rainy, muddy, day and the outside steel door to the crawl space had been off since we moved in. I envisioned all forms of beasties finding their way through the door into the crawl space and somehow up into the house. The door must be closed. There were only two ways to get at it; through the crawl space from an entrance in the garage and another under the deck through a swinging door in the latticework. Since it was like a swamp under the deck, I chose the crawl space route.

Entering from the garage, I looked into this deep, dark, room and wondered if I was doing the right thing. It was an excellent neighborhood for spiders, snakes and other such critters. But, knowing it had to be done, I squeezed through the small entrance into the bottomless pit of this never-land called the crawl space.

Once inside, it wasn't bad. It was dry and relatively clean but very tight as to headroom. I looked over the maze of pipes and ductwork to the other side of the room where I could see daylight through the open door which I had to close. As every story on life after death explains, I went towards the light. Not having a body that fits into European cut suits, I found out, I don't really have a crawl space cut body either.

Eventually, I made it. Unfortunately, I found that to lock the door, you must be on the outside of it. So out I went, under the deck where I could have started.

Sitting in the festering mud, I picked up the big steel door, slammed it shut and closed the two latches. I then turned around and headed for the door in the latticework to get out from this mess.

The door? Where the hell was the door? You could see it easily from outside, but in here, the door was just part of the latticework. I could have kicked out the lattice, but that would have meant my having to put in back together, or face her, Karen-the wife from hell. I think I would rather live under here like some suburban troll.

I finally resorted to my standard solution to such problems. "Karen," I screamed. "Karen" After fifteen minutes of screaming with no responses I knew I was in trouble. Sitting in the mud under my deck brought to mind old World War II movies and the boxes the Japanese used to put prisoners in; the ole black hole.

I started screaming again, "HEEELP...Is anyone up there?" I found out later that they heard me but couldn't find me. They just ran aimlessly from room to room. No one knew where I was, just some disembodied voice screaming, "Help me!"

Eventually, Scott came out on the deck and heard me banging underneath on the deck floor. At first he thought it was some kind of trapped animal, but soon realized it was just me. He confided later that he had fleeting thoughts of negotiating for my release, but soon abandoned them, when he looked under the deck and saw me on all fours sinking into the mud, drooling saliva and cursing. His short-lived victory would have turned into an unprecedented defeat.

He opened the door and out I came, barely able to stand up, and covered head to foot in brown, slimy, mud. Tara standing on the deck looked at me emerging, shrugged and I heard her say to Karen, "Just another typical day in the Barron household."

The normal person might submit to the curse and hire people to come and do such things that might kill them. The normal person might take such incidents as signs of personal shortcomings and the lack of the ability necessary to perform such chores. However, I am not the normal person. It was time to paint the house. I knew this because Karen was being nice to me. She was always nice to me when she anticipated disaster. She never knew which project would be my last. I, of course, took on the challenge myself.

I gathered my tools of destruction; ladder, paint, paintbrushes and first-aid kit and set up everything on the side of the house. I spread out the drop cloth, put on my painting hat and put the hospital emergency room on alert. Now that my entire checklist was complete, I climbed to the top of the ladder and began deciding to do the more difficult section; the overhang first. "Get it out of the way," I reasoned.

In order to reach the overhang, it was necessary to go to the very top of the ladder. To venture above the rung, which says in very clear, bold letters, "Do not go above this step," as I learned that afternoon, was the reason why they put this on ladders.

There I was, perched at the top, joyously painting away on a sunny summer's day, not thinking about much, when suddenly the ground began to shake. I was about twenty feet up, and my world was collapsing beneath me. The ladder was swaying from side-to-side as in some Laurel & Hardy movie.

Finally, after what seemed like an hour, I flew off the ladder as it dropped off to one side. I closed my eyes, tightened my muscles, and waited for the imminent impact with the ground as I planned my route to the hospital. I was braced and ready for the all too familiar pounding to my back, arm or leg. It never came, I never hit the ground.

I was floating, or so it seemed for a fraction of second. What had actually happened was that I had impaled myself through my lower back on a hanging plant bracket. The house had finally gotten even for past abuses. It had made me part of it.

I was suspended, attached to the side of the house. This was embarrassing; this was unique; this was painful. The worst was yet to come however. I must face Mrs. "I told you so." My alternative was to keep still, hang around, and hope to die quickly and rot away before anyone noticed. It was small wonder that mine is the only house in the neighborhood constantly circles by buzzards.

My neighbors, trying to sell their house had some prospective buyers, walking to their front door and they just stopped and stared at me. I smiled and waved as they waved back with mouths open. I would have loved to have heard the explanation of what I was doing there.

It had to be done. "KAREN!" I screamed. "KAREN, I need you!" As always, twenty minutes later she came drifting out. She turned the corner of the house, stared at me for a second and went back in. Was she running for help?

About five minutes later she came back out with the kids. "Look, he figured out something new."

"You don't seem to understand, Karen," I spoke calmly and slowly. "I'm not standing on anything." They just stared at me. No smiles, no tears, no sympathy, just staring. They walked closer, slowly walking around me looking at all angles. They inspected me as you would a fine painting in a museum.

"You finally did it. You finally did something even I can't believe," said my life's partner.

"Can we change our names if this is in the papers?" asked Tara. What a family!

To get me down, it was necessary to have two strong neighbors climb up on ladders and lift me up, over the hook and off. To properly describe the reactions of the two neighbors who rescued me and the emergency room people who tended to me, one must have watched the faces of people looking at the Mona Lisa. Pure, unadulterated awe, a sort of expressionless wonderment.

To me, it was just another day of household chores.

The days of wine and roses continued. I never gave up, I never got better, and I just got more creative. One late winter afternoon it became necessary to go up on the roof to check out the source of a small leak. Going onto the roof is not one of my favorite activities, so I had put it off as long as possible. However, during the last storm, we had so much water in the bedroom I could have stocked the room with trout. The day had arrived, I had to go.

Due to past experiences, I try and avoid ladders whenever possible. I devised a method which I felt was safer. Taking a picnic table onto my rear deck, I placed a picnic bench atop the table. This seemed much sturdier, I felt, and easier to step onto from the roof. So up I went. Not wishing to become a part of any more of my adventures, my family remained in the house.

The trip up wasn't particularly eventful. I scooted up the table, onto the bench, and a short jump later was on the roof. Very proud of myself, I performed my short patch job and it was time to come down. This was where we begin to run into trouble.

The sun was going down and a light chilly breeze was blowing. From the roof, the bench no longer looked like such a large landing site as from down below. In fact, it looked like a runway at 10,000 feet. Sitting on the edge of the roof, I contemplated my next move. Could I reach the bench? Will I miss the bench? Will I miss the table? Will I do significant damage to my body?

The wind was stronger now with an icy bite. I knew I better decide soon. It looked like snow. Gathering all my courage, I turned over onto my belly and let my legs dangle over the roof. I tried to feel the bench below me. Where was it? As I slid lower off the roof, my fingers clutching at the shingles. I couldn't find the bench with my feet. Before I slid past the point of no return, I pulled myself back up onto the roof. The first snowflake hit my nose. I was in trouble!

"Karen!" I shrieked. I needed moral support. "Karen!" Finally, after a long fifteen minutes, she appeared out of the back door. No doubt doing something important like washing floors. "Help get me down!" Consistent with past performance, she wanted to know why I didn't use a ladder like any normal person and went back inside. A real helpmate I thought, as the snow began getting thicker. She'll feel bad when then find my frozen body in the bushes in the morning.

It was a pretty sight. The sun going down over the Putnam County Mountains, the snow falling at a blizzard rate, and a middle-age man lying prone on his roof slowly sliding towards certain death; I must do something soon. If enough snow falls, it won't be my decision anymore.

I stood up, took a deep breath and slid over the edge. I knew eventually I would hit the bench. I just needed faith. I reached my legs lower and lower pushing myself further off the roof. Lower and lower…

It must have been quite an impact when I hit the ground. The next morning I noticed two broken boards on the deck. The front deck and the bench were on the back deck. I had slid off the wrong side of the house.

During the course of my career in home repair I became known as a sort of devil incarnate to the hardware store set. My photo was posted in many of the major outlets as a man to avoid if you want to escape any possibility of being a party to a lawsuit. It was explained to me once that selling me a pair of pliers would appear to a court the same as selling a five year old an Uzi, based on my past history. I was thought of, in effect as the Bob Villa of a negative, parallel, universe. I reached the pinnacle of my reputation one morning in my garage.

One Sunday morning while my family was at the mall, I decided to do some needed work around the garage. Not having a great track record with power tools, or for that matter manual tools, I pulled out my favorite tool, my trusty tube of Super Glue. I truly believed this was the greatest accomplishment in the history of mankind and home improvement. I attacked anything I could glue instead of nailing, since I felt I could do far less damage with my tube as opposed to a hammer. I was wrong!

Somehow, when I put the tube down, it must have leaked out onto the shelf, seeping onto some of the items laying there. The problem was, the next item I picked up had Super Glue all over the handle. The problem was the next item I picked up became a permanent attachment to my hand. The problem was the next item I picked up was a short handled sledgehammer.

So here I stood in the middle of my garage all alone on a Sunday morning with a sledgehammer glued tightly into my clenched left hand. My wife was due home soon and the one question remained, to be caught like this or to cut the hand off at the wrist, claim a chain saw accident, and be out of my misery but retain my dignity.

Remembering that nail polish remover usually released the death grip of Super Glue, I raced to the medicine cabinet, opened it, smashing its mirror, and the wall behind it. I doused my hand and the handle with the polish remover, but my hand was too tightly wedged to the wood. I had no choices left. It was to the hospital or start up the chain saw.

Luckily, the hammer was attached to my left hand as I had a standard shift car and I probably would have beaten myself to death shifting. All I did on the trip over, was crack the driver side window. The only real fear I had, was of being stopped by a policeman for some traffic infraction. Getting out of a car with a sledgehammer in your hand, which you can't put down, would be unnerving even to the most veteran cop. He would have probably shot first and asked questions later.

It is truly amazing, the respect one commands when walking into a hospital emergency room, clutching a sledgehammer. As I sat down at the check-in window, laying my sledgehammer filled hand on the table, the receptionist waived the typical "One moment please while my nails dry…to a shaky…yes sir," while her eyes widened with fear.

Unfortunately, when she heard my sad story, the awe and respect I had garnered to this point, turned to comic relief as word of my predicament spread through the area.

Not surprisingly, I was at the bottom of their triage and I sat for a good two hours in the waiting room trying to look inconspicuous holding my tool. Sometimes when a new group came in, I would walk around tapping beams so they would think I was a contractor.

Eventually, I saw the doctor, who told me he actually had seen much stranger things super-glued to people's bodies, including other nearby body parts. After using a hypodermic needle to get the solvent under the handle, I was extracted and returned in time to beat my family home.

Now that I have added Super Glue to my endangered tool list, I need a new favorite tool. Possibly an arch welder would do it!

14.

REJECTIONS & REJECTED

To commit my life to paper as I have in the preceding pages has been a challenge to me. It was painful, not because I did not want to share the events, but because I did not want to necessarily relive them. If someone doesn't like this epistle they have not liked my life and that may hurt more than the normal rejections; I am a freelance writer. To be precise, this means is that I write things that I think are exceptional, brilliant and resourceful, send them to people who tell me it is incomprehensible, undistinguished and of no earthly concern to anyone, and I go on and write the next piece. This function can best be compared to a television network censor. A necessary evil, but most time completely ignored.

In my single days, if I asked a young lady out and was refused thirty or forty times, I would not go, after each rejection, and change my tie or my hairstyle to try again. Yet this is exactly what we, the freelance writers do, day in and day out. Revise and send, rewrite and mail, I've licked so many stamps I'm hooked on the glue and I can catch flies with my tongue.

Rejection notices can be so masterfully designed that even when they rebuff you you're really not sure if they meant it. They can be so cold-blooded that you feel you're not fit to live and should put yourself out of this misery. I have my favorites at both ends of the spectrum. One publisher sent me a letter as soon as he got the material, telling me how excited he was that I selected him and he cannot wait to read my work. Every two weeks I received another personal letter informing me that he is just so swamped he apologizes, but it is sitting here right on top of his desk and he is trying to wrap up all his other work so he can pounce on mine. Finally, after about two months, I received a letter so well written that you actually feel sorry for the man. His heartbreak in telling you he cannot use the material is so obvious you can almost see little tearstains on the paper. Another publisher sends a Xeroxed postcard after six or seven months telling me that he cannot possibly use this drivel, and that your writing is so bad, he would prefer it if you didn't even buy his magazine.

It is amazing the amount of courses and articles there are for fledgling writers to take advantage of. Book after book of how a particular author made a million dollars in this field. You buy one and read it with awe hoping it will unveil the secrets of the universe and explain to you how to write the great American novel. What you find out is some authors made their million by selling these how to books to neophytes as yourself, and although he professes to know how to, he never did, and he is in the same boat as you except for his advice books.

When I first started this odyssey, everyone told me I had to have a 'writer's market.' This is a book the size of the Little Rock telephone directory, which lists every magazine, publisher, syndicate and agent in the free word by classification of interest. If you happen to have written an article on the Himalayan Wildebeest's adolescent period, there is a publisher that handles that specific topic.

But if you send him a novel documenting exactly what happened to Jimmy Hoffa, he will send it back unopened as it is not his area of interest. Also, every listing seemed to require something called an SASE, yet nowhere in the digest did they ever explain what this was. I went crazy trying to find out. I even wrote to several of the publishers asking them to tell me what this magical item called an SASE was, and how do I go about getting one so I can make a submission to them. Some of them actually wrote back telling me I needed an SASE to get the information I was requesting. I finally garnered enough courage to call one of the publishers, admitted my stupidity and threw myself on their mercy explaining I had no conception of what a SASE was, and could they share this secret with me. I soon found out that SASE stands for "Self Addressed Stamped Envelope."

In essence, a publisher wrote back to me, spending thirty seven cents telling me he couldn't write back to me, because I failed to include a self-addressed stamped envelope. But if I wrote back to him, this time including a self-addressed stamped envelope, he would write back to me, and tell me what an SASE was, so I could write back to him, and send him my manuscript.

And they tell me I am a little strange!

Upon returning from Russia, I assumed the biggest problem I would have was the ultimate selection of my new position from the river of offers that would be thrust upon me; the returning expatriate. With the now international flavor of my resume, I had no doubts, whatsoever, that I would be in great demand.

It is now four months after my triumphant arrival home, and somewhere there is a great dam holding back this river of offers. Not only am I not getting any interviews, lest offers, my rate of rejection letters have dried up considerably. I now become excited when I receive a rejection, as it is a sign that the business community, at least, acknowledges my existence. During the course of my career I have cherished and saved two rejection letters; the first after my application as CFO of the Hopi Indian nation, my rejection was signed by the entire tribal council. (Where is Custer when you need him?), and second, my rejection from Disneyland was a form postcard with Mickey, paws outstretched, and the cartoon balloon verbalizing the Disney organization's complete disgust with my credentials and basically my family tree. There was even some alluding to my never even trying to be a guest at Disneyland again. I'm sure the boys at the post office had a good laugh at this one.

So here I sit, mailing and faxing resumes with abandon. In point of fact, I have mailed so many resumes my postman has recently begun requisitioning a larger truck. After his stop at my home, his deliverable mail had been relegated to the roof of his car. As far as faxing, all that has to be said is that Kinko's has made me 'Customer of the Month' and awarded me their platinum level frequent faxer card which allows me to beat up anyone in front of me on line, and fax at my leisure. Sometimes I even fax a resume, and to be really sure they received it, I mail a second copy. A peripheral benefit of this, of course, is that I now get two reject letters which makes me very happy.

This being the longest period of unemployment I have encountered during my career, I have grudgingly been educated to certain principles which could only be understood and appreciated by those in circumstances such as mine.

PRINCIPLES OF THE TEMPORARILY UNEMPLOYED

1) The workweek should be twenty four hours a day, seven days a week. Weekends and weekdays after 5:00 P.M. are not as attractive to you as when you were employed. Although you are positive the companies to which you have sub-

mitted your resume have people reviewing them twenty four hours a day and seven days a week, you are nevertheless somewhat uncomfortable during these periods. Someone may not be devoting their full attention to your resume during their family Sunday cookout and may miss something.

2) There is one job in every company that was designed for you. Every week in the Wall Street Journal there is, at least, one advertised position that reads as if they had you in mind. Forget the resume and just send in your acceptance letter. You are astounded when you do not even receive one of those prized rejection letters for your efforts. After receiving a rejection letter from IBM on one of these particularly perfect matches, I wrote back to IBM stating I couldn't believe their letter and there must be some mistake. IBM was nice enough to tell me to believe it!

3) The half-life of your resume on an employment agent's desk is approximately two days. The agent has you convinced that they will be concentrating 100% of their time and energy and the combined resources of their entire national and international organization and affiliates to find you a job. The fact is, if a job order is not sitting on their desk at the moment in time they are holding your resume, on day two when you call, you will have to spell your name for them as they have obliterated all memory of you and your resume. It is probably an effective action to resend your resume daily to the agent to rekindle their massive internal operation dedicated to find you a job.)

All in all the process of looking for a new job puts one in the position of utter frustration, hopelessness, helplessness and the feeling that your entire life and future rests on the whim and whimsy of others far less capable than you; I guess it's a lot like being a Democrat.

To most people a resume is a synopsis of your career. A summation, which by convention, is expected to depict positions, education, and other relevant personal facts, all within an acceptable level of truth and accuracy.

This, of course, is the way it's supposed to be. This was not my way. You see, my technique expounds that a resume is dynamic. It is a vibrant, living, breathing chameleon, ever changing its shape, form and content to accommodate the current situation.

Following this approach, I had eight or nine versions of my resume; each custom designed and tailored to the specific advertisement to which I was responding.

Jobs in, jobs out, extend the time here, delete this or that position, creatively describe the duties of one position while upgrading myself in another. This worked very well, except for one particular time, when a small, insignificant little glitch put an end to my technique forever.

I was finally sitting face to face with the senior vice-president of a large bank, which I wanted desperately to join. The bank for which I would have gladly donated one of my kidneys in order to be hired. He picked up my resume from his desk, held it in front of him and said to me, "O.K. Charles. Go ahead and tell me about your career to date."

I was about to open my mouth but suddenly I froze. Which career? Which version of the resume was he holding? I had no idea what the piece of paper in his hand outlining my business life had written on it. I kept no cross reference of to whom I sent what.

My knees turned weak and I started sweating profusely. My eyes must have had the glazed look of a frightened stallion because he asked me in a concerned tone if everything was all right.

I stood up and ambled about the room while talking in generalities. What I was really trying to do was to sneak a peek at the resume he was holding to see what paths my career had taken me. I thought it tacky to ask him if I could see which resume he was holding, so I was attempting to be subtle, yet get a clear look at the document.

At that moment his telephone rang and I took the opportunity of his inattention to lean over his shoulder to get a clear view. I leaned a wee bit too far, lost my balance and all at once I was flat on my back, on his desk looking up at him. So much for subtle. There was no explanation for my Lucille Ball-like escapades where I wound up like a cadaver at a wake with him kneeling along side paying his respects.

The interview went downhill from there. After my acrobatics, I guessed wrong on several positions, even after asking and receiving hints once or twice.

I vowed from then on…to color-code all future mailings!

Since my current job search has not been what you might call productive, I have tried something different. I had discovered that there is a unique service offered to us, the living dead, called job seekers. Basically, the applicant gives this company the parameters of the job they want, and the company plugs this information into a computer, which sends your resume to all advertised positions that fit your description anywhere, it appears in the country. For example, you tell them you want to work in a bank as a teller making $25,000 per year, and every company advertising for a bank teller at $25,000 or more will receive a copy of your resume. It seems like the perfect way to job hunt; no muss, no fuss, no scanning the Wall Street Journal every Tuesday. But leave it to a computer to screw things up.

To date I have received one letter of interest after this massive nationwide mailing of my credentials. What company was it that I impressed? What Chief Executive Officer did I fascinate with my diversity of background? Was it IBM or AT&T? Was it Pepsi Cola International or Shell Oil? Perhaps McDonald's or even the Colonel? No, it was none of these. What it was was Pago, Pago! I received a call from King Pau Pau, his royal majesty of the US possession of Pago, Pago in the American Samoans.

When we relocated to Nashville from New York, we thought a 1000-mile move was an inconvenience. Long distance calls were now necessary to contact friends and family, as was now a plane ride as opposed to a short car trip. Pago, Pago is 8000 miles from California and about two thousand miles southwest of Hawaii. The closest mall is in New Zealand, and New Caledonia, where McHale and his band of merry men hid out during World War II, is within shouting distance.

I now had to tell my family. I had to tell them that the only interview I may be having is with a guy in a sarong who may be offering me poi, pineapples and yams for lunch, instead of martinis and prime rib which I have come to know and love. Karen just stared at me when I broke the news. No screaming, yelling, or crying, no looks of disbelief or amazement. Just the same blank, catatonic stare

I have seen in the past when telling her of other such distinguishable events. Such disclosures as the time I used an indelible marker to connect the freckles on my seven-year-old son's nose and swore it formed the Liberty Bell.

Probably the most noteworthy comment came from my Tara who looked on the bright side and said all of her friends would probably see her quite often; when they film the "Save the Children" commercials. There she would be covered with flies, drinking powdered milk, soulfully waving at the cameras. I admired her optimism.

I concluded my sales pitch to my wife with the fact that if I really shined in the audit position I was discussing with them, if I gave it my all, distinguished myself and ascended through the ranks, someday, although it was too much to hope for, perhaps I would be King Chalee, and you, my lifelong companion, will be "Karen, Queen of the Pago Pagoeans."

15

AGING GRACEFULLY

The surgery before my wedding was the most serious medical problem I have ever had. Outside of some allergy problems, my contact with physicians was rare. The experience of the surgery and some new ailments revealed to me this was a whole new profession within which I could be abused.

One of the results of hitting 60 years of age besides the accumulated wisdom, is the programmed destruction of every operating organ in your body. In a span of only 3 months from my 60th birthday, I was told I had Diabetes, high cholesterol, high blood pressure and a swollen prostate. Three of these were unknown to be, but the fact that I now sleep in the bathroom on army cot, gave me some reason to believe something in that area was amiss.

During a recent visit, my doctor told me I had a cracked rib! The problem was there were no sports, mischief or accidents involved. I obtained this injury by sneezing. An innocent, garden variety, cover-your nose, close your eyes, blessing fetching sneeze. Has my body become so brittle that I can break a bone with a sneeze? Thank God I didn't cough, as I probably would have snapped my head off.

When I was nine, while running after a pop fly, I was hit by a car. After bouncing ten or twelve feet and landing on a fire hydrant, I was still able to catch the ball, and awake the next morning feeling only slightly sore. If that happened today, my entire skeletal structure probably would disintegrate, and they would take my shapeless, jellyfish-like body, pour it into a beaker and take me to the hospital for research purposes.

What happens to our bodies as we age? I no longer can read without glasses, hear without shouts, or eat without heartburn. I'm up when I should be asleep and I'm asleep when I should be up. I freely admit that I am a devout couch potato. In fact, if couch potatoes had their own religion, I would, most certainly be its Pope. But that is no justification for the pain, suffering and indignities one must endure as we get older.

In times past, a doctor's visit would be simple, direct and one to one. He would stand by the table on which I was lying, put a stethoscope to my chest, make me cough, tell me I'm not dying and give me a bill, which I would pay before I left. But things have changed, dramatically. Take as a case in point, my last visit to my family physician 'Dr. D.'

When first calling Dr. D's office for my appointment, I was told the earliest she could see me was in two months. That was fine since it was only an annual physical I was after, but if it had been something serious I, I could have had the hearse drop me off in a couple of months.

After we agreed on the time, the next question wasn't what my complaint was, but rather what insurance company I was with and all of the information needed to process the claim.

I had the feeling that my financial health was infinitely more important to this group than my physical health. After responding to more intense scrutiny than while I was applying for my mortgage, the final question was to name the responsible party to whom they could look in case my multi-billion dollar insurance company went belly up and could not pay their claim. I guess since I was seeing this doctor they weren't to sure about my future ability to handle my own affairs.

The day of my appointment finally came. During my one and a half hour visit, I was subjected to what can only be described as a series of procedures which must have been perfected by the Third Reich.

I was wired up in a harness "The Flying Wallendas" would have been proud of. Then put on a treadmill, and while a beeping machine recorded the calls of help emitting from my innards, I was forced to run a mini-marathon. Only after I collapsed and was dragged off the torture machine by the still churning conveyor, did Dr. D say "O.K. That's enough of this for now."

I was then placed in front of an X-ray plate while a protrusion, I thought I once saw on Flash Gordon's ship, was aimed at my back. All the while I was being told how safe it was by a nurse who was next door in a lead lined observation room wearing a leaded space suit with goggles for extra precautions; The Coupe de Grace was when the nurse, still laden with lead, now donned rubber gloves they use in nuclear reactors to take my blood.

At the end of this fun filled visit, my prognosis was excellent but the charges for the day's activities were larger than the budgets of some third world countries. The paperwork would have given me a hernia if I tried to carry it. They rented me a baggage carrier to take it home.

My doctor these days is an overly cautious, excessively enthusiastic, little Philippino fireball. Not satisfied with treating the overt, diagnosed illnesses we all knew I had and loved, she continually sends me for tests to discover new virgin territories. It is as though she is my agent, and is constantly sending me on "gigs" which I can pass, fail or be recalled for a second tryout. Except in these cases, I pay them. I think my insurance company is hoping for something terminal that will stop this hemorrhaging of their funds.

Recently, she has gone too far, she has sent me to a land where no man has gone before, she has sent me for a Colonoscopy. For the uninitiated, a Colonoscopy is a torture process that was invented by the Nazis during World War II for the purpose of extracting information from prisoners of war. It was then known as the "Upendapooper" or "The Periscope of Pain." It was one of the most effective and horrific procedures. Today, it would be banned by the Geneva Convention as cruel and unusual punishment, however, medical science has renamed it, made it sterile, and calls it "a necessary medical procedure for those over 50 for continued good health." Basically, they lay you out on a table, put you to sleep, and while 5-6 people mill around, they take a 15 foot pipe with a camera, a light and sharp things on the end, and go into an orifice where things should only come out. I always wanted to make it in show biz, but I thought it would be the outside of my body that would be on camera.

To truly understand the total experience you have to start at the beginning, you have to understand, the dreaded "Preparation Day." Since they are going far into your body with this thing that looks like a plumber's snake, it is only common sense that there must be a "clear path" to move along through. How do you make it clear? Aha, here is where the fun starts! The instructions the gastroenterologist's staff gives you are innocent enough;

- On the day before the procedure, you can eat nothing solid, colorful, or with any hint of substance or flavor. You can only drink clear liquids. Nothing Blue, Black, Red or Orange. This leaves basically Lemon and Lime, Jell-O and apple juice. I hate Lemon and Lime anything, as I despise apple juice. When you cannot eat anything, it is truly amazing how may food commercials are on television. I was starving and the incessant food ads were driving me nuts, so to take your mind off of this expected torture, they provide another diversion.

- Then they tell you to go to the drugstore and buy something called Fleet Phospho-Soda. This is an innocuous little bottle with instructions to mix 3 oz of it, with 4 oz of water, and drink at 1:00 P.M. Seems safe enough. What harm could 7 oz of liquid do? First off, it tastes like a Margarita mixed with STP. Salty, oily, lemony and thick. I chased it with apple juice. The issue presented itself in about 20 minutes.

- Try and imagine how your stomach would feel after eating about 2 ½ pounds of flamethrower chili, with some Sea Bass that had been left in the sun for 3-4 days, off a street vendor's cart, on a little side street, in Tijuana. Then double it! It starts mildly enough with some slight bubbling in your gut. You go to the John and do your stuff, and then again. Within an hour, you don't have to worry about those commercials unless you have a TV in your bathroom as you do not see daylight again. At about 4:00 A.M. your socks come out, and it starts to ease up. By now you've lost about 12 pounds of weight, 28 gallons of water, am tired, hungry, weak and still have to go...............for the test.

This is the part I was really worried about. Never having this test before, I was imagining the worst possible scenarios of what the doctor will find up there. I envisioned something akin to a rainforest with birds and mosquitoes, and all sorts of jungle growth, including massive tumors.

I arrived at the doctor's office around 7:00 A.M. leaving everything home, including my reading glasses. Of course, they immediately give me a package of papers to fill out which is only slightly smaller than the congressional report on 9/11. Not being able to read the questions of what I was filling in, I have no idea what diseases I was admitting to, so later when they were all wearing leather overalls, huge rubber gloves, and headgear that one would wear while working with Anthrax spores, I was not really surprised.

I was immediately directed to a small dressing room where I was told to take "everything off" except my socks and shove them into a small plastic bag. As I stood there stark naked, "except for my socks" I felt as if I was about to star in a bad porno movie. Just then, an arm came snaking in through a crack in the door with a dismembered voice instructing me to "put this on." What she handed me was one of the most feared and reviled medical supply there is,.............the rear-opened hospital gown. Nothing, nothing there is can make a strong man cry, a confident man cower. Nothing can make you feel more defenseless and embarrassed than this "garb of shame." While wearing it you do the "hospital shuffle," and walk trying to face everyone, while holding the ventilated back closed and still clutching everything you came with in a non-descript hefty bag.

They then placed me in a lounge chair and told me they had to place the IV connector for the anesthesia. The problem we were now going to have, is the same problem I warn every lab technician about to take any sort of blood test on me, I Have No Veins. A physician once speculated that my body is just filled with blood sloshing around, as I had no visible delivery and transport system for this elixir of life. Challenging this particular nurse, she seemed insulted and said, "I have been doing this for 20 years. You will be no worse than any that I have seen." "OK," I said, and leaned back and watched this impresario with a needle do her stuff. She put a tourniquet on my left arm and twisted it so tight my eyes bulged, but no veins popped out. Next, she put it on my right arm and made it so tight and backed up so much blood, she gave me one of the most massive erections I had ever had. I was ready for sex, but not for seeing some blood. I didn't even have time to bring up this new turn of events as she ran of, and sent the anesthesiologist out, who even after spending at least ten years in school and practice learning how to do this, wound up inserting the needle in the back of my hand, something they really do not like to do.

Finally, they wheeled me into the "procedure room" where I was able to get a good view of "the equipment". It could have easily passed for a small espresso machine, with a ten foot hose for serving and TV screen attached. It was an entertainment center, but unfortunately, I was not the one to be entertained. Within seconds, I was out cold and awoke in the recovery room wondering what sadistic jokes were played out on my body while unconscious.

Within minutes, the doctor came in and anticlimactically told me, "OK, you're squeaky clean. See you in 5 years.' Believe me, I am not complaining he did not find cancer or some other serious disease, but considering everything I had been through to get to this point, at least come out with a dead bird or some discarded plastic casing from a Hebrew National Hot Dog I had swallowed in error.

EPILOGUE

I think of myself as a humorist. I believe I have the ability to look at the most tragic of events and find the humor in it. It is like being a politician. This is becoming more and more difficult as the standard of what is funny is constantly changing and writing with humor is like trying to hit a target on the back of a bucking bronco with a bow and arrow.

It is common knowledge that today's society is much more violent than in year's past. Less obvious though, yet silently evolving in tandem with the changing attitudes toward brutality is the cultural definition of what is funny.

In times past a man slipping on a banana, getting a pie in the face, or wearing a dress a la Milton Berle, was hilarious. Even though the humor was still based on the unfortunate luck of someone, it was mild, mellow and innocuous. Today the humor threshold has unquestionably been dragged forward to actually depend on the misery and suffering of others.

Take, for example, the brutal maiming of John Wayne Bobbit. Thirty years ago the act would have been so heinous as to be virtually unspeakable in the media. Today it is fodder for late night comedians for months on end, ad nauseam.

Political figure's weaknesses in moral or intellectual venues, instead of becoming parameters to gauge their competence, have been relegated to material for television comedy scripts and tee shirt logos.

News of cult standoffs during which the insane actions of authorities and quasi religious leaders resulting in massive losses of lives by fire, sweeps the country not as outrage, but as snappy one liners recounted over lunch.

What exactly is happening? Is it that we are all becoming desensitized to vile acts to where they are funny to us? Is it that as the level of barbarity we are willing to accept as normal, is racing past us so quickly that we cannot keep up with what we should recognize as horror or humor? Or is it that the human mind is just not equipped to deal with such savagery. That in order to protect our sanity and permit us to function in the midst of chaos, a defense mechanism kicks in and permits us to deal with the madness that has become so commonplace.

Whatever it is, this conditioning had better be reversed. We have reached the point where a child's video game depicting one character disemboweling another is considered entertainment played while having his after school milk and cookies. This is a new era and we are creating a generation so blasé and so accepting of evil, that it has given movie producers new challenges in shocking their audiences. Jason is comic relief and the Terminator is outright funny. The Chain Saw Murders are power tool commercials while Jack the Ripper is providing a community service.

It really struck home the other day as I was watching the Alfred Hitchcock classic, *Psycho*. The shower murder scene had given me weeks of nightmares in my teen years, yet my seven year old, who had sneaked in to watch, laughed and thought it was akin to a vaudeville routine.

Where do we go from here? Possibly public executions in comedy clubs?

Next week is my birthday. I know full well that in the cosmic scheme of things, this is entirely inconsequential. I know full well that compared to civil wars all over the planet, nuclear testing and all of the other horrors befalling the masses of humanity, my birthday is a non-event. Yet it is still my own personal abyss from which I must escape.

One may ask, why am I so downhearted about a birthday? I know intellectually that 57 years old is not the end of the line. I understand that I should be thankful that although aside from a few excess pounds, I am physically sound and I am cognizant of the fact that economically I am better off than 80% of the population, yet I am still ruing this big day.

Aside from being a gauge of the place in eternity one occupies during his existence akin to the speedometer of a car, birthdays are also mileposts in your journey through life between which accomplishments should be lined up like little wooden soldiers patiently waiting for a final count. If one was fortunate enough to have been endowed the gift of life from the hall of souls, there must be a final accounting, a justification to determine if during your short spate on earth you were worthy of receiving the bequest in lieu of another. It is this final judgment of which I am apprehensive.

What have I proffered in exchange for my tenure of existence? What have I done to deserve using up the limited resource of a soul? A marriage which produced three children. Are they my contribution? Are one of them destined to be the hope of humanity and my sole job was to give them life, perhaps. During my teaching career, did I touch the heart and mind in one of the students so they would go on and invent the cure for cancer; hopefully? Or was it that during the collision with the millions of human spirits one comes in contact with during the course of a lifetime, I may have unknowingly uplifted their essence, eased their pain or revitalized their vigor. Was this it? Was it enough?

The problem is I have no reason to believe that such an event has ever happened. I have no satisfaction that I have fulfilled my destiny. I have seen no evidence to present at my final calling as to why I was here. As the years fly by, as those mile markers tick off, as my mortality ebbs away into the Netherlands of non-existence, I have done nothing which will live past my being to memorialize my ever having been. I have made no mark nor merited any mention. I will be a ghost without a portfolio.

The time for a new beginning is at hand. Instead of being maudlin at my failures, I should find solace that I still have time to make a change. I still have time to cause a change. I still have time to be changed. I have awoken at this particular birthday to decide that I have been too complacent. I have been more concerned with form than substance, with materiality than charity. I know I can be involved. I know I can make a difference. I know I can be remembered.

Happy Birthday Charley.......

978-0-595-38001-5
0-595-38001-8